Achieving Productivity

Achieving Productivity

24 Essential Skills for High-Performing Teams

Michael Edmondson

BEP

BUSINESS EXPERT PRESS

Leader in applied, concise business books

First published in 2025 by
Business Expert Press, LLC
222 East 46th Street, New York, NY 10017
www.businessexpertpress.com

ISBN-13: 978-1-63742-788-0 (paperback)
ISBN-13: 978-1-63742-789-7 (e-book)

Business Expert Press Human Resource Management and Organizational Behavior Collection

First edition: 2025

10 9 8 7 6 5 4 3 2 1

EU SAFETY REPRESENTATIVE
Mare Nostrum Group B.V.
Mauritskade 21D
1091 GC Amsterdam
The Netherlands
gpsr@mare-nostrum.co.uk

Description

Achieving Productivity: 24 Essential Skills for High-Performing Teams is a customizable learning and development program designed to help individuals and organizations thrive in today's fast-changing global economy.

With disengaged workers, unfilled job positions, and many people living paycheck to paycheck, the modern workforce faces significant challenges. Only 23 percent of workers globally report being engaged at work, while millions of job openings remain unfilled due to a lack of available talent.

The program highlights the importance of adapting to rapid technological changes and emphasizes that success requires more than just technical (hard) or interpersonal (soft) skills. It introduces the concept of Essential Skills, which are critical for connecting and enhancing both hard and soft skills, promoting self-awareness, and helping individuals navigate and succeed in complex environments.

Achieving Productivity offers valuable insights for businesses of all sizes, nonprofits, and government agencies, providing a pathway to develop human capital, boost employee engagement, and ensure long-term success amid ongoing disruptions.

Contents

Introduction

The field of productivity literature remains filled with a tremendous amount of helpful information. The spectrum of advice on achieving productivity generally falls into two distinct yet related paradigms: employees can unlock their productivity by relying on any number of habits. For example, in a January 3, 2024 blog post titled "13 Ways to Enhance Productivity at Work," Natalia Rossingol wrote "productivity is a beast you can control and it depends on various factors, and by carefully considering them, you get an opportunity to work faster and improve your performance."[1] The second paradigm involved with achieving productivity shifts the focus away from the employee and places the emphasis on the leader and their ability to create the proper culture. As Samantha Madhosingh noted in *Forbes*, "the key to unlocking productivity lies not in a rigid stance on work location but in a leader's ability to cultivate an environment of support, flexibility, and empowerment."[2] Both approaches provide important, relevant, and impactful solutions to increase productivity. Moreover, on September 4, 2024, Gallup released insights from its ongoing study of the employee experience. When comparing employee engagement levels, Gallup found that top and bottom quartile business units and teams had a 23 percent difference in profitability.[3] In other words, the more engaged a team the greater the likelihood of increased profitability. Today's volatile, uncertain, complex, and ambiguous (VUCA) global marketplace continues to disrupt almost every aspect of life and work. In order to achieve any level of sustainable growth in today's disruptive, ever-changing, and hyper-competitive VUCA environment, individuals, leaders, and teams need to add another dimension to their commitment to productivity.

Any discussion of achieving productivity needs to include an overview of the state of mind in which workers find themselves. While the literature on this remains vast and continues to grow, here are some key points to remember. Leaders and managers who discount the state of mind in which employees find themselves risk alienating their workforce. Only those leaders and managers who are in tune with the world around them in general, and with their workers specifically, have any hope of achieving productivity.

- According to a Gallup research report published in January 2024, "the percentage of Americans who evaluate their lives well enough to be considered 'thriving' averaged a subdued 52.1 percent."[4]
- When asked the question "Did you experience the following feelings during a lot of the day yesterday?" in the same Gallup poll mentioned just before, 40 percent of Americans reported they worried, while 45 percent acknowledged experiencing stress "a lot of the day yesterday."[5]
- In a November 2023 report published by Lending Club, as of September 2023, 62 percent of adults said that they are living paycheck to paycheck. The report concluded that "living paycheck to paycheck remains the main financial lifestyle among U.S. consumers."[6]
- In its 2023 *State of the Global Workplace Report*, Gallup reported that 23 percent of the global workforce is engaged at work. In the United States specifically, 34 percent of U.S. full- and part-time employees were engaged in their work and workplace.[7]

These four findings from recent research emphasize what leaders and managers need to know and, that is, their people are most likely experiencing some level of financial, physical, social, or emotional stress or worry. Moreover, a January 23, 2024, Gallup report concluded that "in 2023 U.S. employees continued to feel more detached from their employers, with less clear expectations, lower levels of satisfaction with their organization, and less connection to its mission or purpose, than they did four years ago."[8] Sadly, the majority of American workers "are also less likely to feel someone at work cares about them as a person." What do the latest statistics mentioned before have to do with productivity? Actually, quite a bit. Not engaged or actively disengaged employees result in approximately $1.9 trillion in lost productivity.[9] Armed with the latest research data on the level of stress, worry, and engagement among workers, Gallup CEO Jon Clifton was asked: "What can leaders do today to potentially save the world?" Clifton responded with a clear and succinct answer: "Change the way your people are managed."[10] In other words, leaders and managers need to express genuine care about their employees. Unfortunately, if the leader or manager lacks the required self-awareness to care for themselves, it will be difficult if not impossible for them to care for others. That's where *Achieving Productivity* and its 24 essential skills helps.

A team is made up of individuals. Such a basic observation hardly deserves even to be printed. But if we continue to develop that thought, the observation becomes paramount. For example, a team is made up of individuals who find themselves in various positions along the mind-set continuum. The space each team member resides on the continuum between a fixed and growth mindset can impact an organization's capacity to maintain relevance, achieve sustainability, or drive innovation. In today's VUCA environment, it is imperative, in Gallup's words, "to change the way your people are managed" if you want to achieve the level of productivity required to create a sustainable future. Changing the way employees are managed, the following needs to happen.

- Leaders and managers need to recognize that the world is changing. It's a sad reality, but so many do not.
- Leaders and managers need to increase their own self-awareness. Again, it's a sad reality, but many lack even the most basic level of self-awareness.
- Employees need to be encouraged to increase their own self-awareness. Most are hardly given permission to take a vacation day, let alone engage in the word required to increase their own self-awareness.
- Once employees, managers, and leaders have increased their self-awareness, they can then discuss how their views on each of the 24 essential skills impact their work. Only then can an organization move forward and create an environment where the achievement of productivity is possible.

Foreword

In January 2025, two reports detailed the evolving future of work and emphasized human and AI collaboration as essential for success.

The World Economic Forum's Future of Jobs Report 2025 noted, "Helping workers achieve the right mix of technical and human skills will be vital as the future of work continues to evolve." Similarly, LinkedIn's Work Change Report: AI Is Coming to Work concluded, "Companies want talent that will lean into new technology and can learn new technical skills while maintaining strong human skills."

In no particular order, here are 10 key characteristics shaping this New Frontier:

Blended Skillsets: AI and Human Proficiency: Workers need to combine AI literacy with communication, creativity, and leadership. This blend enables effective AI use while preserving the value of human contributions.

Continuous Reskilling and Upskilling: By 2030, 70% of job skills will change. Both reports stress lifelong learning, with LinkedIn users showing a 140% increase in new skill acquisition since 2022.

Adaptive Talent as a Workforce Priority: Adaptability is essential. The Future of Jobs Report highlights resilience and agility as key success drivers, with 38% of executives prioritizing these traits in entry-level hires.

Human-AI Co-creation of Productivity: AI is automating routine tasks, enabling humans to focus on higher-value work. Over 50% of companies using generative AI report a 10% revenue increase.

Creation of New Job Roles: Technological innovation is creating roles like AI Engineer and Data Scientist. In the U.S., 20% of professionals now hold jobs that didn't exist in 2000.

Skills Instability and Transformation: By 2030, 39% of current skills will need updates or will become obsolete. AI-related job postings have increased sixfold in just one year.

Increased Emphasis on Human-Centric Skills: Skills like empathy, ethical judgment, and leadership remain critical. Communication was the most in-demand skill globally in 2024.

Demand for AI Literacy Across Professions: AI skills are now relevant across industries. Non-technical roles like marketing and healthcare have rapidly incorporated AI fluency, with a sevenfold increase since 2018.

Generative AI's Expanding Influence: Generative AI is transforming workflows, enabling less specialized workers to perform expert-level tasks. Currently, 75% of knowledge workers use generative AI.

Shift to a Skills-Based Labor Market: Employers are moving from degree-focused hiring to skills-based assessments. By 2030, 85% of companies plan to prioritize reskilling initiatives.

The Essential Skills outlined here can provide the necessary support for personal development and professional growth as individuals work towards learning, unlearning, and relearning in a world of constant change.

Defining Essential Skills

To achieve a sustainable future in today's VUCA global marketplace, organizations will, according to the 2024 LinkedIn Report, "succeed by embracing growth as a virtuous cycle. Employee growth, through learning and career development, can play a substantial role in an organization's productivity, sustainability, and retention."[1] By embracing the Essential Skills as a foundation of learning and development today, organizations have a new opportunity to modernize their paradigm of employee growth in today's VUCA environment. In a world characterized by rapid technological advancements, economic fluctuations, and sociopolitical uncertainties, the ability to bridge the technical prowess of hard skills with the interpersonal finesse of soft skills through the application of Essential Skills is paramount for success. To achieve productivity today, individuals and teams should identify, assess, and then enhance their Essential Skills. As with both hard skills and soft skills, there are many Essential Skills available for individuals to engage in for their learning and development. The adjacent table defines a few of the many types of each skill category. Essential Skills transcend disciplinary boundaries, emphasize human authenticity, promote self-awareness, and foster an interconnectedness. These characteristics in and of themselves illustrate their difference compared to the hard and soft skills so often discussed in the literature. Essential Skills will continue to grow in significance as the line between humanity and artificial intelligence (AI) develops at unprecedented speed. As Julie Kratz noted in *Forbes*, "human skills are more critical in an AI environment as robots and algorithms rely on human inputs and do not have the ability to process emotions."[2]

HARD SKILLS (PROFESSIONAL DEVELOPMENT)	ESSENTIAL SKILLS FOR LIFE AND WORK	SOFT SKILLS (PERSONAL GROWTH)
Accounting	Abandon impatience to stay dedicated	Active listening
Artifical Intelligence	Adapt and change when necessary	Adaptability and flexibility
CAD/CAM proficiency	Allow yourself to gain a new perspective	Collaboration
Cybersecurity	Assess how you make decisions	Confidence
Data analysis	Challenge your assumptions	Conflict resolution
Database management	Create an authentic sense of self	Cooperation
Digital marketing	Cultivate mental and physical grit	Creativity and innovation
Electrical skills	Design a vision of your future self	Critical thinking
Foreign language proficiency	Develop a growth mindset	Cultural awareness and sensitivity
Graphic design	Embrace VUCA dynamics	Customer service skills
Healthcare expertise	Engage in subtle maneuvers	Decision-making skills
Legal knowledge	Exercise self-discipline	Emotional intelligence
Machine learning	Focus on the present moment	Interpersonal skills
Manufacturing processes	Grow by taking calculated risks	Leadership skills
Mechanical skills	Have a bias towards action	Negotiation skills
Mobile development	Leverage the two dimensions of time	Networking skills
Network administration	Increase your self-awareness	Open-mindedness
Programming	Nurture equanimity in your life and work	Oral Communication
Project management	Practice self-care and self-love	Patience
Quality control	Prioritize respect and thoughtfulness	Presentation skills
Retail merchandising	Rely on positive uncertainty	Problem-solving abilities
Statistical analysis	Remain open to serendipity	Self-motivation and initiative
UI/UX design	Respond with intention and care	Time management
Web development	Understand the dynamics of stress	Written Communication

Another perspective comes from As Nacho De Marco who, in a September 13, 2024, *Fast Company* article, called for the abolition of any labels like hard or soft skills since we "should just call them skills without any qualifiers."[3] In today's world of constant disruption requiring lifelong learning of all types of skills, having the qualifiers like hard or soft adds a layer of unnecessary confusion. While that may be true, the marketplace still uses the terms, and as a result, the paradigm for this publication is that Essential Skills link both the hard and soft skills together forming a necessary bond for employees to succeed.

Transcend Disciplinary Boundaries

Unlike hard skills, which are often specific to a particular domain or industry, and soft skills, which primarily focus on interpersonal interactions, Essential Skills transcend disciplinary boundaries. Essential Skills are fundamental to anyone committed to the belief that if they want to develop as a professional, they will have to grow as a person. They are applicable across generations, titles, functional areas, and industries, making them indispensable for individuals navigating diverse and rapidly changing environments. Whether it's developing a vision for your future self in a world of constant change, relying on your positive uncertainty to think critically, or challenging your own assumptions to communicate effectively with diverse stakeholders, Essential Skills provide individuals with the agility and resilience needed to thrive amidst constant disruption. In today's AI-infused global marketplace, organizations that engage in the necessary skill development of its employees are, according to the Deloitte Human Capital Trends Report, 98 percent more likely to retain high performers.[4]

Emphasize Human Authenticity

Essential Skills play a pivotal role in addressing the evolving demands of the modern workforce. As automation and AI continue to reshape traditional job roles and workflows, there is an increasing emphasis on uniquely human—skills that machines are unable to replicate. Essential Skills, such as creating an authentic sense of self, challenging your own assumptions, and allowing yourself to be vulnerable, are becoming increasingly valued. Authenticity also entails taking responsibility for your choices and actions, being transparent in your dealings with others, and respecting their authenticity as well. It fosters genuine connections and meaningful relationships because people are drawn to authenticity and feel more comfortable being themselves around authentic individuals. In today's VUCA global marketplace, organizations need employees who can couple their authenticity with technology. As Julie Kratz wrote in *Forbes*: "Human skills are more critical in an AI environment as robots and algorithms rely on human inputs and do not have the ability to process emotions."[5]

Promote Self-Awareness

The third characteristic of Essential Skills is that they promote self-awareness. Self-awareness is the capacity to introspectively understand one's own emotions, thoughts, strengths, weaknesses, and motivations. It serves as the compass that guides individuals through the complexities of their environment, enabling them to make informed decisions, manage their reactions effectively, and continuously learn and grow. In the context of Essential Skills, self-awareness acts as a catalyst for fostering a culture of continuous learning and growth. It allows individuals to recognize the need for improvement, identify areas for development, and seek out opportunities for enhancement. By understanding their own learning preferences, cognitive biases, and emotional triggers, individuals can tailor their learning journeys to maximize effectiveness and efficiency. By prioritizing self-awareness and integrating it into their daily practices, individuals can unlock their full potential, thrive amidst change, and contribute meaningfully to the collective journey of growth and development. Employees across all industries, levels, and functions should remind themselves how an increase in self-awareness helps foster a more collaborative and supportive workplace culture, is essential for effective leadership, decision making, communication, and relationship building, and contributes to a productive and harmonious work environment.

One Final Note on Self-Awareness

In a May 2021 *Wall Street Journal* interview, Mark Roellig, who spent his career serving in various capacities across different industries was asked about the process on how an executive develops a leadership philosophy. Roellig, a retired chief legal officer (CLO) and chief technology officer (CTO), emphasized how the development of a leadership philosophy "requires self-awareness, introspection, and empathy. Aspiring leaders need to understand themselves, as well as what it might be like for others working with them. Having a deep-rooted leadership philosophy or guiding principles can help leaders prioritize their interests." Explaining in greater detail, Roellig emphasized how "The one asset none of us can buy more of, fast-forward, or—certainly—rewind is time. Time is our most precious resource, so spend it wisely. How we spend our time is important to happiness, and it demonstrates to others who you are and what you value. Leaders can ask: 'Is the way I spend my time aligned with what I truly value?' If not, fix it."[6] This book is my small attempt to help leaders of all levels increase their self-awareness in order to learn how to align their actions with how they spend their time in the pursuit of leading a high-performing team.

CHAPTER 1

Develop a Growth Mindset

Introduction

To achieve productivity, it is imperative that high-performing teams understand the necessity of, and help foster, the essential skill of developing a growth mindset. As John Muscarella noted, "growth mindset organizations cultivate a high-development culture where employees are empowered to embrace challenges and pursue new knowledge and skills. These organizations are more resilient and adaptable through change and have greater engagement, loyalty, and productivity."[1] On the other hand, "fixed mindset organizations are those that emphasize results and output. These organizations are likely to peak early and plateau quickly."[2] While reflecting on the necessity of learning and that of a growth mindset, Robert Sher noted in *Forbes*, "Without practical planning—and the effort to nurture a growth mindset while teaching their team how to achieve their targets—energy and resources will be unfocused, progress will remain untracked, and the team will never reach its potential."[3] *Fostering a culture of continuous learning within the team, encouraging experimentation, and learning from failures, and providing opportunities for skill development and personal growth are three characteristics of a high-performance team demonstrating a growth mindset.*

Foster a Culture of Continuous Learning Within the Team

Continuous learning serves as the cornerstone upon which high-performing teams build their capacity for agility, innovation, and sustained success. Rather than viewing learning as a sporadic activity, these teams cultivate a culture where learning becomes ingrained in the fabric of everyday operations, shaping a collective mindset of constant improvement and adaptation. Recent research conducted by Deloitte underscores the transformative impact of prioritizing continuous learning within organizations. Their study revealed organizations that place a premium on continuous learning experience a remarkable 37 percent increase in employee productivity and are 92 percent more likely to innovate compared to their counterparts who neglect this aspect.[4] These findings emphasize the pivotal role that learning plays in driving organizational performance and competitive advantage.

In essence, high-performing teams recognize learning as ongoing journey of growth and development. By embracing this mindset, team members become empowered to stay abreast of industry trends, acquire new skills, and challenge conventional thinking. This proactive approach enables teams to anticipate and respond effectively to changing market dynamics, positioning them as frontrunners in their respective industries. A seminal study published in the *Harvard Business Review* further elucidates the benefits of fostering a culture of continuous learning within organizations. According to this study, organizations that prioritize continuous learning are better equipped to navigate uncertainties and disruptions in the marketplace. By fostering a culture of curiosity, exploration, and knowledge sharing, these organizations not only adapt more swiftly to changing circumstances but also outperform their competitors. With an estimated 1.1 billion jobs expected to be disrupted between now and 2030, employees around the world will require upskilling (learning to improve current work) and reskilling (learning to do new types of work).[5]

Organizations such as Walmart and McDonalds are examples of major efforts underway for learning and development. Walmart, for example, is investing $1 billion into reskilling its workforce, and McDonald's has spent $165 million over the past eight years to prepare 72,000 employees for upward mobility. The Association for Talent Development's most recent study found that the average organization spends almost $1,300 per employee on professional learning.[6] It is important to note that many organization spend far less per employee, and unfortunately, some organizations spend little to no money on educating employees. Leaders who would like to help their organizations remain vital, vibrant, and relevant, should remember how a culture of continuous learning fosters an environment where creativity and innovation flourish. When team members are encouraged to explore new ideas, experiment with different approaches, and learn from both successes and failures, they are more likely to generate groundbreaking solutions and drive organizational growth. This aligns with research findings that highlight the positive correlation between a learning culture and innovation output. Ultimately, the significance of continuous learning extends beyond individual skill development—it permeates every aspect of organizational performance. From enhancing employee engagement and retention to fostering adaptability and innovation, the benefits of prioritizing continuous learning are manifold. By embracing a culture of continuous learning, high-performing teams position themselves as dynamic, resilient, and forward-thinking entities capable of thriving in today's rapidly evolving business landscape.

Encourage Experimentation and Learning From Failures

Experimentation lies at the heart of innovation and growth within high-performing teams. These teams recognize that to stay ahead in a constantly evolving landscape, they must be willing to push boundaries, try new approaches, and take calculated risks. Unlike traditional paradigms where failure is stigmatized, high-performing teams embrace a mindset where failure is not seen as a setback but as an invaluable learning opportunity. Research conducted by Google's Project Aristotle underscores the importance of psychological safety in fostering a culture of experimentation and learning from failures. Psychological safety refers to the belief that one can take risks within a group without fear of negative consequences to their self-image, status, or career. In essence, it is the foundation upon which trust, openness, and collaboration thrive within teams.

As researchers have noted, "Psychological safety is the bedrock of high-performing teams."[7] This sentiment underscores the pivotal role that psychological safety plays in enabling teams to innovate and thrive. When team members feel psychologically safe, they are more likely to share their ideas, voice their concerns, and take risks without fear of embarrassment or retribution. In a psychologically safe environment, team members are encouraged to experiment, challenge the status quo, and learn from both successes and failures. Rather than being met with criticism or punishment, failures are viewed as opportunities for reflection, growth, and improvement. This fosters a culture of resilience, adaptability, and continuous improvement within the team. Moreover, psychological safety encourages open communication and constructive feedback, which are essential for fostering collaboration and driving innovation. When team members feel safe expressing their opinions and share their perspectives, it leads to richer discussions, better decision making, and ultimately, superior outcomes. In practical terms, fostering psychological safety requires intentional efforts from team leaders and members alike. Leaders must create an environment where trust, respect, and vulnerability are encouraged, while also setting clear expectations for behavior and performance. This may involve establishing norms for communication, providing opportunities for team bonding and rapport-building, and actively listening to and addressing concerns raised by team members.

Provide Opportunities for Skill Development and Personal Growth

Investing in the development of team members is not merely a discretionary expense for organizations; rather, it is a strategic imperative that underpins long-term success and competitiveness. High-performing teams recognize the intrinsic value of skill development and personal growth, understanding that empowered and skilled employees are indispensable assets in achieving organizational goals. By prioritizing the professional development of their workforce, these teams create a virtuous cycle of growth, innovation, and talent retention. As highlighted by a report from LinkedIn, a staggering 94 percent of employees express a willingness to stay longer at a company that invests in their career development. This statistic underscores the significant impact that investment in employee development has on organizational loyalty and retention. When employees perceive that their organization is committed to their growth and advancement, they are more likely to remain engaged, motivated, and dedicated to their work.

Furthermore, high-performing teams recognize that talent development is not a one-time event but an ongoing process of continuous improvement. By providing opportunities for training, mentorship, and career advancement, organizations foster a culture of learning and growth that permeates every aspect of their operations. These initiatives not only enhance individual skills and competencies but also cultivate a sense of collective purpose and cohesion within the team. Josh Bersin, a renowned human resource analyst, aptly notes, "Organizations that invest in employee development not only attract top talent but also experience higher levels of employee engagement and productivity." This observation underscores the symbiotic relationship between employee development, engagement, and organizational performance. When employees feel valued, supported, and empowered to grow, they are more likely to demonstrate higher levels of commitment, innovation, and productivity. Moreover, investing in employee development serves as a powerful tool for talent attraction and retention. In today's competitive labor market, organizations that prioritize employee growth and advancement are better positioned to attract top talent and retain high-performing employees. By offering opportunities for professional development, mentorship, and career progression, organizations differentiate themselves as employers of choice, thereby strengthening their talent pipeline and competitive advantage. Investing in the development of team members is a strategic imperative for high-performing teams. By prioritizing skill development and personal growth, organizations foster a culture of continuous improvement, talent retention, and organizational success. As evidenced by research findings and expert insights, organizations that invest in employee development reap tangible benefits in terms of employee engagement, productivity, and talent attraction. In today's dynamic and competitive business environment, investing in employee development is not just a best practice—it is a prerequisite for sustained growth and prosperity.

Conclusion

Fostering a culture of continuous learning, experimentation, and skill development is imperative for cultivating high-performing teams. Continuous learning serves as the bedrock upon which teams build their capacity for agility, innovation, and adaptation. By embracing a mindset of constant improvement and adaptation, teams position themselves as frontrunners in their industries, equipped to anticipate and respond effectively to changing market dynamics. Moreover, psychological safety plays a pivotal role in fostering experimentation and learning from failures, enabling teams to innovate and thrive. When team members feel empowered to take risks, share ideas, and learn from their experiences without fear of negative consequences, it creates an environment where resilience, collaboration, and innovation flourish. High-performing teams understand that in today's fast-paced business environment, the only constant is change, and, therefore, continuous learning and adaptability are essential elements for success.

Additionally, investing in skill development and personal growth is essential for nurturing talent retention and driving organizational success. By providing opportunities for training, mentorship, and career advancement, organizations foster a culture of continuous improvement and talent retention, positioning themselves as employers of choice in today's competitive labor market. Employees who feel supported in their professional growth are more likely to remain engaged, motivated, and committed to the organization's goals. Furthermore, embracing a culture of experimentation encourages innovation and drives progress within high-performing teams. Rather than fearing failure, team members are encouraged to test new ideas, iterate on existing processes, and explore unconventional solutions. This willingness to take calculated risks fosters creativity and allows teams to uncover new opportunities for growth and improvement. As Henry Ford famously said, "Failure is simply the opportunity to begin again, this time more intelligently." High-performing teams understand that failure is not the end but rather a stepping stone toward greater success.

Moreover, effective communication remains paramount in fostering collaboration, alignment, and problem-solving within high-performing teams. Open communication channels and feedback loops enable teams to share information, exchange ideas, and address challenges in real time. When team members feel comfortable expressing their thoughts, concerns, and suggestions openly, it cultivates a culture of transparency and trust. This open dialogue encourages diverse perspectives and leads to more innovative solutions. The quote "without communication, there is no relationship; without respect, there is no trust; without trust, there is no teamwork" comes to mind here. Attributed to different people throughout history, this observation highlights the fact that cultivating high-performing teams requires a multifaceted approach that encompasses continuous learning, experimentation, skill development, and effective communication. By fostering a culture that prioritizes these elements, organizations empower their teams to adapt, innovate, and achieve remarkable success in today's rapidly evolving business landscape. As the world continues to change, high-performing teams should remind themselves of the necessity to remain agile, resilient, and ready to embrace the challenges and opportunities that lie ahead.

Self-Reflection Questions

1. How do I currently perceive challenges and setbacks in my work? Do I view them as opportunities for growth or as obstacles to avoid?

2. In what ways can I contribute to fostering a culture of continuous learning within my team?

3. How do I encourage my team members to embrace experimentation and learn from failures without fear of negative consequences?

4. What steps can I take to stay abreast of industry trends and continuously acquire new skills relevant to my role?

5. How can I help create an environment of psychological safety where team members feel comfortable sharing their ideas and taking risks?

6. What opportunities for skill development and personal growth are currently available to me, and how can I take advantage of them?

7. How do I contribute to open communication and constructive feedback within my team? Are there ways I can improve in this area?

8. How do I currently approach continuous improvement in my work, and what strategies can I implement to enhance this mindset?

9. In what ways do I support my team members' professional development, and how can I do more to help them grow?

10. How can I balance the focus on results and output with the necessity of nurturing a growth mindset within my organization?

CHAPTER 2

Adapt and Change When Necessary

Introduction

To achieve productivity in today's hyper-competitive global marketplace, an organization should consider practicing the essential skill of encouraging employees to adapt and change when necessary. Doing so, and encouraging employees, to adapt and change is generally considered one of the most difficult skills to practice and achieve for an organization. As Jorrit de Groot noted in a December 11, 2024 *Forbes* article "Organizational change is notoriously challenging, with up to 70% of change initiatives failing" https://www.forbes.com/sites/sap/2024/12/11/how-ai-is-transforming-change-management/. The relationship between organizational productivity and the ability to adapt and change when necessary is fundamental in today's dynamic business environment. Researchers Martin Reeves and Mike Deimler argue that "adaptability is becoming increasingly crucial for organizational success in their article. They emphasize that in a rapidly changing world, businesses must be agile and responsive to shifting market conditions, technological advancements, and evolving customer preferences."[1] This proactive approach to change enables organizations to stay ahead of the curve and maintain high levels of productivity in the face of uncertainty. In a December 2023 interview, John Santagate, Vice President of Robotics at Körber Supply Chain Software, elaborated on the pace of change organizations can expect in 2024 and the necessity for companies to adapt. Referring to the supply chain industry specifically, Santagate explained how the industry "has been in a state of transformative change over the last decade—and next year, the pace will only accelerate, especially with the advent of sophisticated technologies like artificial intelligence and the continued investment in modern robotics."[2] Creating a culture of flexibility and agility within the team, encouraging open communication and feedback loops, and promoting a willingness to embrace change and try new approaches are three characteristics of a high-performance team adapting and changing when necessary.

Creating a Culture of Flexibility and Agility Within the Team

High-performing teams exhibit a keen awareness of the indispensability of flexibility and agility in navigating the complex and ever-evolving terrain of modern business. Rather than being tethered to rigid plans or processes, these teams embody a culture of adaptability, characterized by the ability to pivot swiftly and decisively in response to shifting circumstances and emerging opportunities. According to a recent report by McKinsey & Company, teams that prioritize flexibility and agility demonstrate a distinct advantage in their capacity to respond adeptly to market shifts and evolving customer needs. This advantage affords them the ability to maintain a competitive edge in dynamic environments, where agility often spells the difference between success and stagnation. The insights from McKinsey's report underscore the transformative potential inherent in fostering a culture of flexibility and agility within teams. In their *Wall Street Journal* article, Rick Wartzman and Kelly Tang echoed similar sentiment and wrote "executives at the most-effective companies tend to be tolerant of ambiguity and adaptable, according to new research conducted by the Drucker Institute."

By instilling a mindset of adaptability, organizations empower their team members to embrace change as an opportunity rather than a threat. Such empowerment encourages individuals to think creatively, explore innovative solutions, and adapt swiftly to novel circumstances. In essence, fostering flexibility and agility cultivates a resilient workforce—one capable of not only weathering the storm of uncertainty but also thriving amidst its challenges. As far back as 2011, the *Harvard Business Review* published research that concluded: "Increasingly, managers are finding that a sustainable competitive advantage stems from the organizational capabilities that foster rapid adaptation. Instead of being really good at doing some particular thing, companies must be really good at learning how to do new things."[3] In 2025, a world markedly different than 2011, high-performing teams will need to understand this imperative implicitly and prioritize flexibility and agility as cornerstones of their approach to work.

Indeed, the ability to adapt is no longer a mere advantage but a prerequisite for survival in today's hypercompetitive landscape. High-performing teams that recognize this reality position themselves strategically by fostering a culture that celebrates agility and flexibility. In doing so, they equip themselves with the tools and mindset necessary to confront uncertainty head-on, transforming adversity into opportunity and change into growth. As organizations continue to navigate the complexities of the modern business environment, the cultivation of flexibility and agility within teams emerges not merely as a strategic choice but as an existential imperative—one that paves the way for sustained relevance and success in an ever-changing world.

Encouraging Open Communication and Feedback Loops

Effective communication serves as the cornerstone of high-performing teams, acting as the lifeblood that fuels collaboration, alignment, and problem-solving. In the fast-paced landscape of modern workplaces, where agility and responsiveness are paramount, open communication channels and feedback loops are essential components that enable teams to thrive. At the heart of effective communication lies the ability to share information, exchange ideas, and address challenges in real-time. When team members are encouraged to voice their perspectives openly and transparently, it creates an environment where ideas can flow freely, leading to innovation and creative problem-solving. Moreover, open communication fosters a sense of inclusivity and belonging within the team, empowering every member to contribute meaningfully to the collective goals. Central to this is the ability of leaders to demonstrate incredible people skills. As John Marcante, former global CIO at Vanguard, noted "leaders with emotional intelligence, cognitive flexibility, and creativity can persuade, influence, and mentor."

Research conducted by McKinsey concluded that well-connected teams can increase productivity by 20 to 25 percent.[4] Think Talent and CMS Wire uncovered how organizations with effective communication strategies were 3.5 times more likely to outperform their peers.[5] These findings emphasize the significance of establishing robust communication infrastructure within teams, as it enables them to navigate uncertainties and changes in their environment with agility and resilience. Furthermore, effective communication goes beyond just conveying information—it cultivates a culture of transparency, trust, and accountability within teams. When team members feel comfortable expressing their thoughts, concerns, and suggestions without fear of judgment or reprisal, it fosters a sense of psychological safety. This psychological safety encourages individuals to take risks, share innovative ideas, and collaborate more effectively, ultimately driving the team toward success.

In today's VUCA-driven global marketplace, open channels of communication are a prerequisite in order to help all team members maintain clarity, focus, and understanding with the goal of deepening collaboration and enhancing decision making. Additionally, constructive feedback, when communicated effectively, helps teams identify areas of improvement, encouraging continual learning and performance enhancement. High-performing teams prioritize open dialogue and constructive feedback, recognizing that it is through honest and candid conversations that they can identify opportunities for improvement, address challenges proactively, and adapt to changing circumstances. In practical terms, fostering effective communication within teams requires deliberate effort and intentionality from both leaders and team members. Leaders play a crucial role in setting the tone and establishing communication norms within the team.

By modeling transparent communication, actively soliciting feedback, and creating opportunities for open dialogue, leaders can create an environment where communication flourishes. Moreover, investing in tools and technologies that facilitate communication and collaboration can significantly enhance team effectiveness. Whether it's through project management platforms, messaging apps, or video conferencing tools, leveraging technology can break down communication barriers, especially in remote or distributed teams. However, effective communication is not solely the responsibility of leaders—it requires active participation and commitment from every team member. Each individual must prioritize active listening, empathy, and clarity in their communication efforts. By seeking to understand diverse perspectives, respecting differing opinions, and communicating with clarity and purpose, team members can contribute to a culture of open communication and collaboration.

Promoting a Willingness to Embrace Change and Try New Approaches

In today's rapidly evolving business landscape, change is not just a possibility but a constant reality. High-performing teams recognize this fundamental truth and approach change not with trepidation but with enthusiasm, viewing it as an opportunity for growth and innovation. Rather than being paralyzed by uncertainty or clinging to outdated methods, these teams embrace change as a catalyst for progress and transformation. A study conducted by the Center for Creative Leadership reinforces the notion that embracing change is a hallmark of high-performing teams.[6] The study revealed that teams willing to embrace change and explore new approaches are not only more likely to achieve breakthrough results but also to sustain long-term success. This underscores the transformative power of cultivating a culture of innovation and adaptability within teams, where change is seen as an opportunity rather than a threat.

Promoting a culture of innovation and adaptability requires more than just lip service—it demands a fundamental shift in mindset and approach. Organizations must encourage team members to adopt a mindset of curiosity, experimentation, and continuous improvement. This involves creating an environment where individuals feel empowered to challenge the status quo, explore new ideas, and take calculated risks. By fostering a culture of innovation, organizations create a fertile ground for creativity and ingenuity to thrive. Rather than stifling creativity with rigid processes or hierarchical structures, high-performing teams encourage open-mindedness and exploration. They understand that innovation often arises from unexpected sources and are willing to entertain ideas that may initially seem unconventional or risky.

Steve Jobs, the visionary co-founder of Apple Inc., famously emphasized the importance of innovation in distinguishing between leaders and followers. He understood that innovation was far more than creating new products or services, as it also involved fundamentally reshaping industries and challenging the status quo. High-performing teams embrace this philosophy, recognizing that innovation is not just a goal but a mindset—an ongoing commitment to pushing boundaries, disrupting norms, and driving change. Embracing change as an opportunity for innovation requires more than just a willingness to try new things—it requires a culture of trust, collaboration, and resilience. Team members must feel supported and empowered to take risks, knowing that failure is not only accepted but embraced as an essential part of the learning process. Leaders play a crucial role in creating this environment, providing guidance, support, and encouragement as teams navigate uncharted territory. Furthermore, high-performing teams in today's hypercompetitive, dynamic, and ever-changing global marketplace understand that innovation is a continuous journey. They recognize the importance of ongoing learning and adaptation, constantly seeking feedback, iterating on ideas, and refining processes. This iterative approach allows teams to stay agile and responsive in the face of evolving challenges and opportunities.

Conclusion

High-performance teams that prioritize creating a culture of flexibility and agility recognize the ever-changing nature of markets, technologies, and customer needs. As Chad Wachter noted in a *Forbes*, April 2023 article, "markets, technologies and customer needs are constantly evolving. If you want to stay competitive and relevant, you need to be willing to adapt and evolve as well. This means being open to new ideas, taking calculated risks and experimenting with different approaches."[7]

By fostering an environment where team members are encouraged to embrace change and try new approaches, these teams position themselves to thrive amidst uncertainty. This requires a willingness to challenge the status quo, take calculated risks, and experiment with innovative ideas. Embracing change not only enables teams to seize new opportunities but also enhances their resilience in the face of unforeseen challenges. Encouraging open communication and feedback loops is another key aspect of creating a high-performance team. Effective communication serves as the linchpin that fosters collaboration, alignment, and problem-solving. When team members feel empowered to share their thoughts, concerns, and suggestions openly, it cultivates a culture of transparency and trust. Feedback loops ensure that communication remains ongoing and constructive, allowing teams to continuously improve and adapt. By prioritizing open dialogue, high-performance teams can harness the collective intelligence of their members, leading to more innovative solutions and better outcomes.

Moreover, promoting a willingness to embrace change and try new approaches is essential for driving innovation and growth. In today's fast-paced business landscape, complacency is a recipe for stagnation. High-performance teams understand the importance of remaining agile and responsive to emerging trends and opportunities. This requires a mindset of curiosity and experimentation, where failure is viewed not as a setback but as a valuable learning experience. By encouraging team members to step out of their comfort zones and explore new ideas, organizations foster a culture of innovation that propels them ahead of the competition. In conclusion, high-performance teams that embody a culture of flexibility, open communication, and innovation, position themselves for long-term success. By adapting to changing circumstances, embracing new ideas, and fostering a collaborative environment, these teams not only stay competitive but also drive continuous growth and improvement. As the business landscape continues to evolve, the ability to navigate uncertainty and seize opportunities will be crucial for maintaining relevance and achieving sustainable success.

Self-Reflection Questions

1. How do I currently respond to changes and new challenges in my work environment? Do I see them as opportunities for growth or as threats to stability?

2. In what ways can I contribute to creating a culture of flexibility and agility within my team?

3. How can I encourage open communication and feedback loops to ensure that all team members feel heard and valued?

4. What steps can I take to stay updated on market shifts, technological advancements, and evolving customer preferences relevant to my role?

5. How can I foster an environment where team members feel comfortable experimenting with new approaches and learning from failures?

6. How do I balance the need for stability with the necessity of adapting to change in my day-to-day work?

7. What strategies can I implement to improve my ability to pivot swiftly and decisively in response to emerging opportunities or challenges?

8. How can I support my team members in developing a mindset of curiosity, experimentation, and continuous improvement?

9. How do I currently contribute to promoting a culture of innovation and adaptability within my organization? Are there areas where I can improve?

10. What practical steps can I take to enhance psychological safety within my team, ensuring that everyone feels empowered to share ideas and take risks without fear of negative consequences?

CHAPTER 3

Develop a Vision for Your Life

Introduction

In the dynamic landscape of contemporary workplaces, high-performing teams standout for their exceptional outcomes as well as for their profound understanding of the importance of personal and collective growth. These teams exhibit a distinctive trait: they actively engage their members in designing a vision of their future selves. Jan Torrisi-Mokwa, author of the book *Building Career Equity*, discusses some of the many reasons why high-performing teams should encourage employees to develop a vision for their lives. According to Torrisi-Mokwa, employees should develop career equity as it is a "framework that provides tools and strategies to keep people on a path toward doing engaging work and fulfilling the careers and lives they envision."[1] One example of a tool is the concept of a three-year letter that employees write to their future selves as it often has a powerful effect on one's professional *and* personal growth. This chapter delves into the rationale behind why high-performing teams prioritize this practice, focusing on three specific traits: establishing clear team goals aligned with a shared vision, encouraging individual team members to set personal development goals, and fostering a sense of purpose and direction within the team. Drawing from recent insights, this discourse aims to shed light on the profound impact of these practices on team dynamics and overall performance.

Establish Clear Team Goals With an Alignment Toward a Shared Vision

High-performing teams understand that clarity in goals and objectives is crucial for success. By aligning team goals with a shared vision, they create a roadmap that guides their collective efforts and ensures that everyone is working toward the same end. This alignment is not merely about setting targets, but involves a comprehensive process of defining the team's mission, values, and long-term aspirations. Such a process requires input from all team members to ensure that the vision resonates with everyone and that there is a collective buy-in. As researchers Greg Satell and Cathy Windschitl noted: "In today's disruptive marketplace, every organization needs to attract, develop, and retain talent with diverse skills and perspectives. The difference between success and failure will not be in the formulation of job descriptions and compensation packages, but in the ability to articulate a higher purpose."[2] To that end, Satell and Windschitl noted the importance of leadership providing a clear sense of shared mission and values. "Managers must clearly communicate their organization's shared mission and hire people who will be inspired to dedicate their talents to it. The art of leadership is no longer merely to plan and direct action, but to inspire and empower belief."[3]

The creation of a shared vision involves several key steps. First, it requires effective leadership to articulate a compelling and achievable vision. Leaders must communicate this vision consistently and convincingly, ensuring that it is understood at all levels of the team. They need to explain the rationale behind the vision and how it aligns with the organization's broader goals. This communication should be an ongoing process, reinforced through regular team meetings, updates, and feedback sessions. In the event that external or internal events should impact the vision, the leader then has a responsibility to update it and share that with the team. Second, the development of a shared vision involves collaborative goal setting. Team members should be encouraged to contribute their ideas and perspectives, making the vision a collective creation rather than a top-down directive. This participatory approach fosters a sense of ownership and accountability among team members. When individuals feel that they have a stake in the vision, they are more likely to be committed to achieving it. Third, aligning goals with a shared vision requires continuous monitoring and adjustment. Teams must regularly review their progress toward the vision and make necessary adjustments to stay on track. This involves setting measurable milestones, tracking performance, and providing feedback. Regular reviews help ensure that the team remains focused and that any deviations from the vision are promptly corrected.

The potential impact of a clearly articulated shared vision on team dynamics could be profound. It has the opportunity to foster a sense of unity and direction, making it easier for team members to collaborate effectively. When everyone is working toward a common goal, there is less room for misunderstandings and conflicts. Team members are more likely to support each other, share knowledge, and work synergistically. This collaborative environment enhances the overall productivity and efficiency of the team. Moreover, a shared vision provides a sense of purpose and meaning to the work. Team members are not just completing tasks but are contributing to a larger cause. This sense of purpose can be a powerful motivator, particularly during challenging times. When the team faces obstacles, the shared vision serves as a reminder of why they are doing what they are doing, helping them to stay resilient and focused.

As early as 2006, researchers noted the Volatile, Uncertain, Complex, and Ambiguous (VUCA) dynamics two decades ago and stressed the need for teams to establish clear team goals with an alignment toward a shared vision. In the *Psychological Science in the Public Interest* journal, researchers wrote "A variety of global forces unfolding over the last two decades, however, has pushed organizations worldwide to restructure work around teams, to enable more rapid, flexible, and adaptive responses to the unexpected. This shift in the structure of work has made team effectiveness a salient organizational concern."[4] Sixteen years later, in 2022, Abbie Lundberg echoed similar sentiment when she wrote about the disruptive dynamics of uncertainty during the 2020s. According to Lundberg, with the extraordinary demands on organizations today, "effective leaders must have courage and a strong sense of purpose and be able to adapt to rapidly changing circumstances. Many of the biggest challenges call less for vision and the ability to inspire—the historically vaunted hallmarks of leadership—and more for being able to consider new perspectives and test new approaches to getting work done."[5]

Encouraging Individual Team Members to Set Personal Development Goals

In addition to setting team goals, high-performing teams emphasize the importance of personal development. By encouraging team members to set individual goals, they create an environment that supports continuous growth and improvement. In a February 2024 *Forbes* article, Martha Jeifetz highlighted the critical role personal development goals play in a team setting. According to Jeifetz, leaders have a responsibility to champion a diverse culture that embraces risk while valuing failure as a stepping stone toward success. Such a culture "involves creating a trusting and safe environment where everyone within the team can thrive and contribute their best. In this way, the team journey becomes not just a pursuit of goals but a collective adventure that enhances individual and collective potential and long-term business results."[6]

Moreover, personal development in team settings is crucial. When team members have the chance to develop their skills and pursue their interests, it creates a more innovative and dynamic team environment. Given the fact that Gallup research published in 2024 found 31 percent of employees are actively engaged at work, this focus on personal growth benefits individuals and fosters a culture of continuous learning and adaptability within the team. This continuous learning and adaptability remains a critical imperative since, as *The Wall Street Journal* noted in 2023, "Managers and employees spend more than 75 percent of their time engaged in collaborative activities, and having a strong team is crucial to corporate performance and worker satisfaction."[7]

Fostering a Sense of Purpose and Direction Within the Team

A sense of purpose is a powerful motivator that drives high-performing teams to excel. By fostering a shared sense of purpose, these teams create an environment where members feel connected to something larger than themselves. Leaders who create a caring culture and cultivate a strong sense of purpose are more resilient and adaptable, able to navigate challenges with greater ease. This sense of purpose not only enhances team cohesion but also boosts individual morale, commitment, and resilience. As researchers noted: "Resilience is an essential trait for leaders to cultivate within teams to help them navigate workplace challenges effectively. As senior leaders steer employees through uncertain terrain, a team dynamic that allows team members to bounce back from challenges and overcome obstacles together can be the difference between organizational success and failure."[8] By modeling openness, acknowledging limitations, and fostering genuine connections, leaders can empower their teams to beat adversity with strength, adaptability, and resilience.

Conclusion

In today's dynamic workplaces, high-performing teams excel not only in their outcomes but also in their commitment to both personal and collective growth. By actively involving team members in envisioning their future selves, these teams create a framework that fosters innovation and adaptability. Central to this approach is the alignment of clear team goals with a shared vision, which guides collective efforts and ensures unified direction. Additionally, encouraging individual team members to set personal development goals nurtures a culture of continuous growth, contributing to both individual and team success. A strong sense of purpose further enhances team cohesion, driving members to connect their work to a larger cause and navigate challenges with resilience. Together, these practices highlight the profound impact of personal and collective growth on team dynamics and performance, underscoring the importance of investing in both for organizational success.

Self-Reflection Questions

1. How well do I understand the shared vision and goals of my team?
2. In what ways have I contributed to the development and alignment of our team's mission and values?
3. How often do I set personal development goals that align with our team's objectives?
4. What steps have I taken to actively engage in envisioning my future self within the team?
5. How does my personal growth contribute to the overall success and dynamics of my team?
6. In what ways do I foster a sense of purpose and direction in my work and within my team?
7. How effectively do I communicate and reinforce our team's shared vision to my colleagues?
8. What strategies do I use to support and encourage my team members in their personal development goals?
9. How do I ensure continuous monitoring and adjustment of our team's progress toward its vision and goals?
10. How resilient and adaptable am I in navigating challenges and changes within my team and organization?

CHAPTER 4

Exercise Self-Discipline

Introduction

Author E.B. White once wrote: "If the world were merely seductive that would be easy. If it were merely challenging, that would be no problem. But I arise in the morning torn between a desire to improve (or save) the world and a desire to enjoy (or savor) the world. This makes it hard to plan the day."[1] The individuals and teams who achieve productivity exercise self-discipline to improve the world and enjoy it simultaneously. It is not an either-or decision for those who understand that self-discipline is the cornerstone of success in any endeavor, and its importance is magnified in the context of high-performing teams. It should also be said that pursuing both (enjoying and improving the world) require one to work hard at hard work. Doing so in not for the faint of heart. Within such teams, the ability to exercise self-discipline manifests in various forms, each crucial for achieving collective goals and maintaining peak performance. This chapter explores three key traits related to exercise self-discipline in high-performing teams: setting clear priorities and goals, establishing routines and systems, and holding team members accountable.

Setting Clear Priorities and Goals for the Team

Setting clear priorities and goals within a team serves as a strategic imperative for an organization as it works toward a common destination. This alignment is about coordinating tasks and harmonizing individual energies and talents toward a shared vision. In a *Wall Street Journal* article, Tim Smith noted that "leaders can help clear a path to success and empower their people to break through siloes and the status quo."[2] J. Eric Pike, CEO of Pike Enterprises, a North

Carolina-based infrastructure solutions provider is one example of a leader who understands the need to set clear priorities and help his employees stay focused. According to Pike, "My role was to simply not let the organization back up, to continue to pump the vision of where we needed to be. And if anyone presented a roadblock, I told them to go under, over, through, around—any way to make it happen."[3] In the dynamic landscape of modern business, where uncertainty is the only constant, clarity of purpose becomes paramount. Clarity of purpose serves as a catalyst for a team as it works to overcome one challenge after another in today's disruptive marketplace. High-performing teams leverage this clarity as a strategic advantage, enabling them to navigate complexities with confidence. When the destination is crystal clear, the path forward becomes evident, and teams can chart their course amidst uncertainty with a sense of purpose and direction.

Moreover, setting clear priorities and goals fosters a culture of ownership and accountability within the team. When team members understand the overarching goals and their roles in achieving them, they develop a sense of ownership over their tasks and responsibilities. This ownership goes beyond mere compliance; it becomes a driving force propelling individuals to go above and beyond, fueled by a personal stake in the team's success. In high-performing teams, ownership is not relegated to a select few but permeates throughout the team's fabric. Each member takes pride in their contribution, knowing that their efforts directly contribute to the team's collective success. This sense of ownership instills a culture of accountability, where commitments are honored, and deadlines are met without the need for external enforcement. When everyone is aligned toward a common purpose, accountability becomes intrinsic, driving the team toward excellence. In essence, setting clear priorities and goals within a team is not just about defining objectives; it's about shaping a shared destiny. It empowers teams to harness the power of clarity amidst chaos, fostering a culture of ownership and accountability that propels them toward their aspirations. As high-performing teams embrace this principle, they harness the transformative potential of self-discipline, turning aspirations into achievements and goals into reality.

Establishing Routines and Systems to Maintain Focus and Productivity

Routines and systems serve as the backbone of high-performing teams, providing the necessary framework for success in an increasingly complex and demanding world. Like the scaffolding of a towering structure, these routines and systems offer stability, consistency, and support, allowing teams to navigate challenges and reach new heights of productivity and excellence. James Clear's assertion that "You do not rise to the level of your goals. You fall to the level of your systems" encapsulates the pivotal role that routines and systems play in the achievement of goals.[4] Goals alone are not enough; it is the systems, coupled with the organizational culture, in place that determine the trajectory of progress. In the context of teams, this rings particularly true, as the collective efforts of individuals must be orchestrated and coordinated through effective systems to achieve desired outcomes.

In a world inundated with distractions, the ability to maintain focus is a scarce and valuable asset. Cal Newport's insight that "The ability to concentrate intensely is a skill that must be trained" underscores the deliberate effort required to cultivate focus amidst a sea of distractions.[5] High-performing teams recognize this skill as essential and invest in building routines and systems that foster and protect concentration. Whether it's implementing time-blocking techniques or creating designated focus zones, these teams understand that sustained focus is the cornerstone of productivity and innovation. Moreover, routines and systems instill discipline and habituation within teams, fostering a culture of consistency and excellence. By embracing routines and systems, high-performing teams transcend the limitations of individual effort, harnessing the collective power of consistency and discipline. These teams recognize that success is not a result of chance but a product of deliberate and systematic effort. As they cultivate focus, endurance, and discipline, they pave the way for sustained excellence and achievement. In a world where change is constant and challenges are abundant, these routines and systems provide the anchor that keeps high-performing teams steady amidst the storm.

Holding Team Members Accountable for Their Commitments and Deadlines

Accountability stands as the cornerstone of high-performing teams, serving as the bedrock upon which trust, responsibility, and excellence are built. When a leader holds him/her self and everyone equally accountable, and clearly articulates the vision and everyone's role in the process, then the level of responsibility is apparent to each individual. In the dynamic environment of teams, characterized by fast-paced changes and evolving challenges, this ability to respond to commitments and challenges is indispensable for achieving collective goals. High-performing teams understand that accountability transcends hierarchical structures; it is a collective responsibility shared by all members. To remain vibrant, vital, and relevant in today's VUCA global marketplace, leaders need to practice what David Brooks labeled "ethical leadership" which is "deeply humanistic."[6] Doing so allows the leader to put "people over process, and deeply honor those right around them" in order to provide candid and direct communication within teams.[7] In such teams, accountability is not enforced through authoritarian measures but is rather embraced as a guiding principle that drives continuous improvement and excellence. Team members hold themselves and each other to high standards, recognizing that constructive feedback is essential for personal and collective growth.

Furthermore, accountability serves as a catalyst for trust and cohesion within teams. When team members hold themselves and each other accountable for their actions and commitments, trust flourishes naturally. This trust forms the foundation upon which genuine collaboration and innovation thrive, enabling high-performing teams to achieve extraordinary results. In high-performing teams, accountability is not viewed as a burden but as a privilege—a testament to the team's commitment to excellence and mutual respect. Through accountability, team members demonstrate their dedication to the collective vision, ensuring that every action is aligned with the team's goals and values. This shared sense of accountability fosters a culture of ownership, where individuals take pride in their contributions and hold themselves accountable for their impact on the team's success. Ultimately, accountability is more than just a mechanism for tracking progress; it is a mindset—a commitment to integrity, transparency, and excellence. In high-performing teams, accountability is woven into the fabric of everyday interactions, serving as a guiding principle that propels the team toward its highest aspirations. As team members embrace their individual and collective responsibilities, they lay the groundwork for sustained success and lasting impact.

Conclusion

In conclusion, high-performing teams excel by striking a balance between improving and enjoying the world, grounded in the fundamental practice of self-discipline. This discipline is essential for setting clear priorities and goals, establishing effective routines and systems, and holding team members accountable for their commitments. Clarity of purpose guides teams through uncertainty, fostering ownership and accountability among members. Routines and systems provide the structure necessary for maintaining focus and productivity in a distracting world. Accountability, as a shared responsibility, builds trust and drives continuous improvement. Together, these elements create a culture of excellence, enabling teams to transform aspirations into achievements and navigate challenges with confidence and cohesion.

Self-Reflection Questions

1. How do you balance the desire to improve the world with the need to enjoy it?
2. What personal strategies do you use to maintain self-discipline in your daily life?
3. How do you set clear priorities and goals for yourself and your team?
4. What routines and systems have you established to maintain focus and productivity?
5. How do you ensure accountability within your team or group?

6. In what ways do you foster a sense of ownership and accountability among team members?
7. How do you navigate uncertainties and disruptions in your work or personal life?
8. What methods do you use to cultivate intense concentration and minimize distractions?
9. How do you handle roadblocks or challenges that arise in the pursuit of your goals?
10. How do you integrate the principles of ethical leadership and humanistic values in your interactions with others?

CHAPTER 5

Cultivate Mental and Physical Grit

Introduction

In the ever-evolving landscape of organizational dynamics, the cultivation of mental and physical grit emerges as a cornerstone for achieving and sustaining high performance within teams. These teams, marked by their resilience, support, and celebration of determination, navigate challenges with fortitude and emerge stronger from adversity. Noting the critical role grit plays in high-performing teams, Michael Teti, managing partner at Digistream Investigations acknowledged his experience at the company where he had been on teams with and without grit. Teti started at Digistream as an entry-level employee and worked his way up to the C-suite. According to Teti, "the one constant has been the presence of grit in the best-performing teams. From my perspective, grit has been critical in achieving success. This realization has reinforced my belief in the importance of incorporating and practicing gritty attributes daily for my teams."[1] This chapter delves into three critical traits of cultivating mental and physical grit—promoting resilience and perseverance, providing comprehensive support, and celebrating instances of determination—underscoring their symbiotic relationship with high-performing teams.

Promote Resilience and Perseverance in the Face of Challenges

Resilience and perseverance serve as the foundation for the success of high-performing teams, acting as catalysts for growth, innovation, and sustained excellence. Resilience is not merely about bouncing back from adversity but also about bouncing forward, learning, and growing from the experience. This perspective reframes challenges as opportunities for personal and collective development, emphasizing the transformative power of resilience within teams. High-performing teams actively promote resilience and perseverance among their members, recognizing their paramount importance in navigating complex and unpredictable environments. Great teams do not shy away from adversity; instead, they lean into challenges with determination and resolve. This proactive stance highlights the willingness of resilient teams to confront obstacles head-on, viewing setbacks as opportunities for innovation and improvement rather than insurmountable barriers. As noted "in today's rapidly evolving workplace, resilience is a crucial skill that empowers individuals to navigate challenges, bounce back from setbacks and maintain high performance. Building resilience enhances your ability to adapt to change, promotes well-being, and encourages a positive work environment."[2]

Furthermore, resilience fosters a culture of psychological safety within teams, enabling individuals to take calculated risks and explore new ideas without fear of judgment or reprisal. A growth mindset plays a crucial role in thriving amidst challenges, viewing failure not as evidence of unintelligence but as a springboard for growth. By fostering a growth-oriented mindset, high-performing teams cultivate a sense of resilience that empowers members to embrace uncertainty and ambiguity with confidence and determination. In essence, resilience and perseverance are integral to the fabric of high-performing teams, enabling them to navigate adversity, foster innovation, and sustain excellence. By embracing challenges as opportunities for growth, these teams actively promote a culture of resilience and perseverance, resilience among members, and fostering a culture of psychological safety and growth mindset, teams lay the foundation for enduring success in today's dynamic and competitive landscape.

Practice Psychological and Physical Health

The well-being of team members stands as a cornerstone for sustaining high performance and productivity within any organization. On Adam Grant's TED podcast WorkLife, Harvard professor Amy Edmondson described psychological safety as "a climate in which one feels one can be candid." Edmondson explained that the workplace where psychological safety is practiced "is a place where interpersonal risks feel doable, interpersonal risks, like speaking up with questions and concerns and half-baked ideas and even mistakes."[3] Grant emphasized how the opposite, a workplace that fails to practice psychological safety is where people get grilled and reprimanded or even punished for voicing concerns. Such a negative work environment often finds employees saying different things behind leaders' backs than to their faces. A workplace with high psychological safety, however, invites openness, collaboration, and those in turn help innovation thrive since employees feel comfortable and empowered to share ideas, even if they deviate from the norm.[4]

Recognizing the intricate connection between physical and mental well-being, it is essential to understand that physical well-being serves as the foundation upon which mental resilience is built. This underscores the importance of providing resources for maintaining physical health within high-performing teams. By offering access to fitness facilities, wellness programs, and stress management resources, teams empower their members to prioritize self-care and achieve a harmonious balance between their personal and professional lives. Integrating comprehensive support for mental and physical well-being is vital for sustaining peak performance within high-performing teams. Creating a culture of support that embraces vulnerability, empathy, and authenticity fosters an environment where individuals feel valued and empowered to prioritize their well-being. Moreover, providing resources for maintaining physical health lays the groundwork for enhancing mental resilience and sustaining excellence amidst the challenges of the modern workplace. Ultimately, a focus on holistic well-being enables teams to thrive and maintain high levels of productivity and innovation.

Celebrate and Recognize Instances of Resilience and Determination Within the Team

Celebrating instances of resilience and determination within a team not only acknowledges individual efforts but also reinforces their significance within the team culture, inspiring continued excellence and commitment. As noted in a blog entry on Intrafocus: "Celebrating team victories, no matter how small boosts morale and confidence. Teams that regularly take time to acknowledge and appreciate their accomplishments collectively are more confident in their abilities to succeed. This confidence, in turn, fuels their resilience in overcoming adversities."[5] Moreover, celebrating instances of resilience and determination cultivates a sense of collective achievement and camaraderie within teams. By highlighting examples of individual and collective perseverance, high-performing teams foster a culture of collaboration and mutual support, where each member's contribution is celebrated and acknowledged. In essence, celebrating instances of resilience and determination serves as a powerful tool for reinforcing their significance within the team culture and inspiring continued excellence and commitment among team members. By recognizing and honoring individual and collective efforts, teams foster a culture of appreciation, gratitude, and camaraderie, driving sustained motivation and engagement toward shared goals and objectives.

To help celbrate and recognize instances of resilience and determination within the team, the leader should seek out and share success stories. Communicating those stories to internal and external audiences can further demonstrate how the leader is commited to practicing the essential skill of cultivating mental and physical grit. When and where possible, the leader or management team should provide rewards and incentives so that employees understand, even on a small scale, how the organization appreciates those who exercised the required mental and physical grit to get something done. Additionally, creating opportunities for fun and socialization, both online and offline, can help boost morale and motivation. Ultimately, celebrating the achievements and progress of a team can help reinforce the utility of the essential skill of resilience. .

Conclusion

In the evolving landscape of organizational dynamics, cultivating mental and physical grit is essential for achieving and sustaining high performance within teams. High-performing teams, characterized by resilience, support, and a celebration of determination, navigate challenges with fortitude and emerge stronger from adversity. This chapter explores three critical traits for cultivating mental and physical grit: promoting resilience and perseverance, providing comprehensive support, and celebrating instances of determination. Resilience and perseverance form the foundation for success, enabling teams to view challenges as opportunities for growth. Integrating support for mental and physical well-being is vital, as a culture of support, vulnerability, empathy, and authenticity fosters an environment where individuals feel valued and empowered. Recognizing the connection between physical and mental well-being, providing resources such as fitness facilities and wellness programs enhances resilience. Celebrating resilience and determination within the team acknowledges individual efforts and reinforces their significance, fostering a sense of collective achievement and camaraderie, which drives sustained motivation and engagement toward shared goals.

Self-Reflection Questions

1. How do I currently demonstrate resilience and perseverance in my daily work?
2. In what ways can I foster a culture of psychological safety within my team?
3. How do I balance my physical and mental well-being to maintain high performance?
4. What strategies can I implement to help my team navigate challenges with determination and resolve?
5. How can I contribute to creating an environment that values and prioritizes well-being and self-care?

6. What steps can I take to promote a growth mindset within my team?

7. How do I recognize and celebrate instances of resilience and determination within my team?

8. In what ways can I support my team members in taking calculated risks and exploring new ideas?

9. How can I ensure that my team views setbacks as opportunities for growth and innovation?

10. What actions can I take to reinforce the importance of grit and resilience in achieving team success?

CHAPTER 6

Increase Your Self-Awareness

Introduction

Increasing one's self-awareness is the next essential skills individuals and teams should consider practicing in order to achieve productivity. In her 2018 book *Insight: The Surprising Truth About How Others See Us, How We See Ourselves, and Why the Answers Matter More Than We Think,* organizational psychologist Tasha Eurich details how self-awareness is the meta-skill of the 21st century. According to Eurich, self-aware people are more successful, confident, and build better relationships with internal and external stakeholders. After spending several years studying how self-awareness impacts organizational behavior, she concluded that "our self-awareness sets the upper limit for the skills that make us stronger team players, superior leaders, and better relationship builders."[1] High-performing teams are not solely defined by the skills and abilities of individual members but also by their collective self-awareness. Self-awareness within teams entails understanding one's strengths, weaknesses, values, and impact on others. This chapter explores how three key aspects of increasing self-awareness—encouraging reflection and introspection, providing opportunities for feedback and self-assessment, and fostering an environment of honesty and transparency—contribute to the success of high-performing teams.

Encouraging Reflection and Introspection Among Team Members

Encouraging team members to engage in reflection and introspection is akin to providing them with a compass to navigate the complexities of teamwork. Steve Jobs's remark during his 2005 Stanford University commencement speech: "Your work is going to fill a large part of your life, and the only way to be truly satisfied is to do what you believe is great work. And the only way to do great work is to love what you do," serves as a beacon guiding individuals toward aligning their personal values with their professional endeavors.[2] This alignment delves deep into the core of one's being, necessitating introspection. In the context of teams, encouraging such introspection isn't just about self-discovery; it's about unlocking the collective potential within the group. When individuals take the time to reflect on their passions, strengths, and values, they gain clarity on how these attributes intersect with the team's objectives. This clarity empowers them to contribute more effectively, leveraging their unique strengths in service of shared goals. Moreover, introspection breeds empathy and understanding among team members, fostering a profound sense of camaraderie and mutual respect. As individuals become more attuned to their own aspirations and struggles, they naturally become more empathetic toward the experiences of their colleagues. This heightened empathy forms the bedrock of strong team dynamics, where each member feels valued and understood.

Psychologist Carl Rogers eloquently captured the transformative power of self-acceptance in personal growth with his statement, "The curious paradox is that when I accept myself just as I am, then I can change."[3] This quote encapsulates the profound truth that true change arises from a place of self-acceptance. In the context of teams, encouraging individuals to embrace their strengths and weaknesses creates a culture of psychological safety—a space where vulnerability is not only accepted but celebrated. In such an environment, team members feel empowered to acknowledge their limitations and seek opportunities for growth without fear of judgment. This openness paves the way for authentic collaboration, as individuals bring their whole selves to the table, unencumbered by pretense or insecurity. By fostering a culture of reflection, introspection, and self-acceptance, teams cultivate an environment where each member can thrive and contribute meaningfully. This process isn't just about improving individual performance; it's about elevating the collective consciousness of the team, propelling them toward greater heights of success and fulfillment. As team members embark on their journey of self-discovery, they not only unlock their own potential but also forge deeper connections with their colleagues, laying the foundation for enduring collaboration and shared achievement.

Providing Opportunities for Feedback and Self-Assessment

High-performing teams are like finely tuned machines, constantly striving for excellence through a culture of reflection, continuous learning, and improvement. In such an environment the expectations are clear, the job descriptions updated as needed, and the approach transparent. Albert Bandura's insight, "Self-efficacy is the belief in one's capabilities to organize and execute the courses of action required to manage prospective situations," underscores the transformative power of self-assessment.[4] By fostering self-efficacy, self-assessment enables individuals to take ownership of their growth and performance within the team, driving a sense of agency and accountability. In the dynamic landscape of teamwork, where challenges are ever-present and circumstances are in flux, the combination of feedback and self-assessment forms the bedrock of a culture of accountability and continuous improvement.

By offering opportunities for both external feedback and internal reflection, high-performing teams create an environment where learning is ingrained in the fabric of everyday interactions. This iterative process of feedback and self-assessment enables team members to adapt swiftly to changing circumstances and challenges, driving collective success. The leadership itself also needs to be assessed by the employees in a manner in which anonomyity is paramount for the workers. Ultimately, by prioritizing continuous learning and improvement through feedback and self-assessment, high-performing teams unlock their full potential, propelling themselves toward ever-greater heights of achievement. As team members embrace a mindset of growth and development, they not only elevate their own performance but also contribute to the collective success of the team, forging a path toward sustained excellence.

Fostering an Environment of Honesty and Transparency in Self-Evaluation

Honesty and transparency form the bedrock of trust within teams, fostering an environment where open communication thrives. An oft-quoted phrase, attributed to different people, is applicable here and states: "The truth is, unless you let go, unless you forgive yourself, unless you forgive the situation, unless you realize that the situation is over, you cannot move forward." Such a belief serves as a powerful reminder of the importance of acknowledging reality in self-evaluation. This quote illustrates how the notion of true progress can only be achieved when individuals are willing to confront the truth, no matter how uncomfortable it may be. Within the context of teams, fostering honesty creates a safe space where members can confront difficult truths and address underlying issues constructively. By embracing transparency, teams can openly discuss mistakes and setbacks, viewing them not as failures but as opportunities for learning and growth.

By creating a culture of honesty and transparency in self-evaluation, teams lay the foundation for trust and cohesion. When individuals feel empowered to speak openly about their experiences and challenges, trust flourishes, enabling teams to navigate obstacles with resilience and grace. Moreover, by embracing vulnerability, team members cultivate empathy and understanding, strengthening the bonds that unite them. In essence, honesty and transparency in self-evaluation are essential for building trust and fostering open communication within teams. By acknowledging reality and embracing vulnerability, teams create a culture where individuals feel valued, supported, and empowered to achieve collective success. As team members lean into honesty and transparency, they not only elevate their own performance but also contribute to the growth and resilience of the team as a whole.

Conclusion

Increasing self-awareness is essential for individuals and teams to achieve productivity. Tasha Eurich, in her book, *Insight: The Surprising Truth About How Others See Us, How We See Ourselves, and Why the Answers Matter More Than We Think,* emphasizes self-awareness as a crucial skill for success and effective leadership. Self-awareness within teams involves understanding personal strengths, weaknesses, values, and their impact on others. This chapter highlighted three key aspects to enhance self-awareness: encouraging reflection and introspection, providing opportunities for feedback and self-assessment, and fostering an environment of honesty and transparency. Encouraging introspection helps team members align their values with team goals, fostering empathy and understanding. Feedback and self-assessment drive continuous improvement and accountability. Lastly, honesty and transparency build trust, enabling open communication and resilience within teams.

Self-Reflection Questions

1. How can increasing self-awareness contribute to your personal and professional success?
2. In what ways can self-awareness help you build better relationships with colleagues?
3. How do your strengths, weaknesses, and values align with your team's objectives?
4. What strategies can you use to encourage reflection and introspection within your team?
5. How can feedback and self-assessment be integrated into your team's daily interactions?
6. What are some practical steps to foster a culture of honesty and transparency in your team?
7. How can self-acceptance lead to personal growth and improvement within a team context?
8. In what ways does introspection breed empathy and understanding among team members?

9. How can embracing vulnerability and openness improve team dynamics and collaboration?
10. What are the benefits of creating a psychologically safe environment where team members can acknowledge their limitations and seek growth opportunities?

CHAPTER 7

Engage in Subtle Maneuvers

Introduction

The essential skill of engaging in subtle maneuvers might, at first, seem counter to helping a team achieve productivity. By definition, subtle maneuvers refer to the work someone engages in outside of their normal daily responsibilities. To understand the nuances involved with this essential skill, it is important to define the two spheres of subtle maneuvers: company focused and individual focused. Subtle maneuvers focused on the company allow an employee to work on a project outside of their normal scope of work. Successful case studies of this include Google where one policy permitted employees to spend 20 percent of their time on interesting and new projects unrelated to typical daily operations. Two examples born from the subtle maneuvers of Google employees were Gmail and AdSense. Known simply as the "20 percent time" policy, Google sadly abandoned its policy in the fall of 2023. Fortunately, other companies maintain a policy that encourages employees to engage in work-related projects outside of the scope of their daily operations. For example, LinkedIn has InCubator, Apple has Blue Sky, and Microsoft created The Garage. Projects created through subtle maneuvers offered by these policies generally only benefit the company. High-performing teams, however, have the opportunity to engage in the essential skill of encouraging their employees to practice subtle maneuvers in order to follow their own pursuits outside of normal business hours.

THE BENEFIT OF SUBTLE MANEUVERS

Encouraging employees of high-performance teams to have outside interests can be immensely beneficial for both the individuals and the team as a whole. For example, engaging in activities outside of work can stimulate creativity and foster innovative thinking. Pursuing hobbies or interests unrelated to their professional roles exposes employees to new ideas, experiences, and perspectives. They may draw inspiration from their outside interests and apply fresh insights to their work, contributing to the team's ability to generate innovative solutions and approaches. Additionally, encouraging outside interests promotes a healthier work–life balance for employees. Engaging in activities they enjoy outside of work helps employees recharge, reduce stress, and prevent burnout. A balanced lifestyle contributes to overall well-being and productivity, enabling team members to perform at their best when they are at work. Moreover, outside interests often involve developing skills and competencies that may not be directly related to employees' professional roles. Whether it's learning a musical instrument, mastering a sport, or volunteering for a cause, these activities provide opportunities to acquire diverse skill sets and experiences. Recent research published in the *Harvard Business Review* explicitly stated that organizations should give employees "greater power to define their work hours" they need to pursue their passions.[1] "Passions may require employees to commit to specific times and are predicated on regular attendance. Employees need to know they shouldn't feel guilty about leaving work or have to wonder whether doing so will jeopardize performance reviews."[2]

THE LITERATURE OF SUBTLE MANEUVERS

Three books examine this lifestyle. Jon Acuff's book, *Quitter: Closing the Gap Between Your Day Job & Your Dream Job*, examines the possibility and reality of translating an idea for a new product or service into a dream and not a nightmare while balancing the demands of a full-time employment position. Mason Currey's book, *Daily Rituals: How Artists Work* examines dozens of creative people and concludes most of them engaged in subtle maneuvers to pursue meaningful creative work while also earning a living. "The book makes one thing abundantly clear: There's no such thing as the way to create good work, but all greats have their way." In *Real Artists Have Day Jobs: (And Other Awesome Things They Don't Teach You in School)*, Sara Benincasa proclaimed that "the biggest myth we are fed as artists is that we need to sustain ourselves solely on our art. This is ridiculous. Every artist has at some point in time had some other job. Some of them kept these jobs their entire lives." There is no need to be a starving artist because many successful artists held day jobs. Working during some part of the day was common place for artists of the past and continues to be so today.

EXAMPLES OF PROFESSIONALS WHO ENGAGED IN SUBTLE MANEUVERS

Here are five of the many artists who held day jobs to help finance their art.

- Frank O'Hara published *Lunch Poems* as a series of reflections he made from his work at the Museum of Modern Art.
- T.S. Eliot wrote *The Waste Land* by night and worked accounts at Lloyds Bank during the day.
- Wallace Stevens won the 1955 Pulitzer Prize in poetry. When Harvard University offered him a faculty position, he declined it since it would have required him to give up his vice-presidency of The Hartford insurance agency where he supervised real estate claims.
- Richard Serra is an American minimalist sculptor who started a furniture removals business in New York called, Low-Rate Movers. He employed many of his fellow struggling art friends, including artist and composer Philip Glass, who worked as his assistant helping him to install shows and move furniture.
- Sujatha Gidla published *Ants Among Elephants* in 2017 while working as a conductor for the New York City subway.

These five artists, and many others, engaged in subtle maneuvers to produce their art and work a day job. German-language novelist and short story writer Franz Kafka, widely regarded as one of the major figures of 20th-century literature, relied on subtle maneuvers. Most successful people who navigate the chaos use the subtle maneuvers strategy. Throughout his life, Kafka had a Brotberuf—a bread job that allowed him to have a reliable source of income. Franz Kafka's father often referred to his son's job at the Worker's Accident Insurance Institute as his Brotberuf— a job to put bread on the table. Kafka's job with Worker's Accident Insurance Institute had him investigate and assess compensation related to personal injury cases involving lost fingers or limbs, to name just a few of the many situations. Kafka usually got off work at 2 p.m., so that he had time to spend on his literary work. Kafka described his approach to writing in a letter to a friend: "Time is short, my strength is limited, the office is a horror, the apartment is noisy, and if a pleasant, straightforward life is not possible, then one must try to wriggle through by subtle maneuvers." Kafka was unknown during his own lifetime, but he did not consider fame important. He became famous soon after his death. Almost all of Kafka's work incidentally was published posthumously, against his wishes. Kafka is renowned for his visionary and profoundly enigmatic stories that often present a grotesque vision of the world in which individuals burdened with guilt, isolation, and anxiety make a futile search for personal salvation. His major works include: The Trial (Der Prozess), The Castle (Das Schloss), Amerika, and The Metamorphosis. Kafka had a full-time job, yet used subtle maneuvers to write at night and on the weekends. American composer Charles Edward Ives leveraged subtle maneuvers as well.

Ives is widely regarded as one of the first American composers of international significance. Unfortunately, Ives's music was largely ignored during his life, and many of his works went unperformed for many years. To support his family, he maintained a long career in the insurance business. As Ives put it, if a composer "has a nice wife and some nice children, how can he let them starve on his dissonances?" Encouraged by his father to experiment with music, became a church organist at the age of 14, and wrote various hymns and songs for church services. After graduating from Yale in 1898, he secured a position in New York as a $15-a-week clerk with the Mutual Life Insurance Company. In 1899, Ives moved to employment with the insurance agency Charles H. Raymond & Co., where he stayed until 1906. In 1907, upon the failure of Raymond & Co., he and his friend Julian Myrick formed their own insurance agency Ives & Co., which later became Ives & Myrick, where he remained until he retired. He achieved considerable fame in the insurance industry with many of his business peers surprised to learn that he was also a composer. In his spare time, he composed music and, until his marriage, worked as an organist in Danbury and New Haven as well as Bloomfield, New Jersey, and New York City.

CONCLUSION

Encouraging employees of high-performance teams to have outside interests promotes creativity, work–life balance, diverse skill sets, broader networks, increased engagement, and resilience. By supporting employees' holistic well-being and personal development, organizations can cultivate a thriving and resilient workforce capable of achieving exceptional results collaboratively. Remember, supporting employees' outside interests demonstrates how an organization values a holistic well-being and personal development approach. Employees feel appreciated and respected when they are encouraged to pursue their passions and interests outside of work. This can lead to higher levels of engagement, job satisfaction, and morale within the team, fostering a positive and supportive work environment. As Stephanie Burns wrote in *Forbes*, engaging in subtle maneuvers is important for employees "from a holistic perspective. Focusing on a passion that has nothing to do with your 9–5 or what pays the bills can actually enhance your performance at work, make you happier, and make you more creative."[3]

Self-Reflection Questions

1. What activities or projects outside of your normal daily responsibilities are you passionate about, and how do they inspire you?
2. How do you currently balance your professional responsibilities with your personal interests or hobbies? Do you find this balance fulfilling?

3. Have you ever participated in a company-focused subtle maneuver (e.g., a project outside your usual scope)? If so, how did it impact your creativity and job satisfaction?

4. What individual-focused subtle maneuvers (e.g., personal projects or hobbies) do you engage in outside of work, and how do they contribute to your overall well-being?

5. How do activities outside of work stimulate your creativity and foster innovative thinking in your professional role?

6. In what ways do your outside interests help you achieve a healthier work–life balance? How does this balance affect your productivity at work?

7. What new skills or competencies have you developed through your personal interests or hobbies, and how have they enriched your professional capabilities?

8. How have your outside interests helped you expand your social networks? Have these connections led to any new opportunities or collaborations at work?

9. Are there any individuals (e.g., artists, professionals) who successfully balanced their day jobs with their passions that you look up to? How do their stories resonate with your own experiences?

10. Considering the benefits of engaging in subtle maneuvers, how do you plan to incorporate more of these activities into your life? What long-term goals do you have that align with these pursuits?

CHAPTER 8

Abandon Impatience to Stay Dedicated

Introduction

In today's fast-paced world, where technology and information flow at unprecedented speeds, high-performing teams are often under immense pressure to deliver quick results. This demand for rapid outcomes can lead to a culture of impatience, where short-term gains are prioritized over sustainable, long-term success. However, for teams to thrive and achieve enduring success, they must learn to balance this pressure with a strategic focus on lasting objectives. Abandoning impatience is not just a necessity but a cornerstone for maintaining dedication and reaching ambitious goals. High-performing teams that embrace patience and persistence are better equipped to handle the inevitable setbacks and challenges that arise on the path to success. Patience allows teams to stay the course even when immediate results are not visible, while persistence ensures continuous effort and progress toward long-term objectives. Moreover, focusing on incremental progress rather than immediate results helps teams stay motivated and maintain momentum. Small, consistent steps forward can accumulate into significant achievements over time, providing regular opportunities for recognition and reinforcement of effort. Finally, fostering a culture of perseverance and commitment within the team creates an environment where dedication and resilience are valued and nurtured. When leaders model these behaviors and encourage open communication, team members feel supported in their efforts to overcome obstacles and stay committed to their goals. By implementing these three tactics—cultivating patience and persistence, focusing on incremental progress, and fostering a culture of perseverance and commitment—teams can navigate challenges more effectively and ensure consistent performance.

Cultivate Patience and Persistence in Pursuit of Long-Term Goals

Patience and persistence are fundamental to achieving long-term objectives. In a world that often emphasizes immediate results, teams that prioritize these qualities are uniquely positioned to handle setbacks and maintain focus on their overarching mission. There is an often-used maxim that applies here: "life is a marathon, not a sprint." This perspective underscores the necessity of a long-term view, where steady progress and resilience become the pillars of success. Patience is the ability to endure delays and obstacles without losing sight of the ultimate goal. As Benjamin Laker wrote in *Forbes*: "Every significant achievement in life requires a degree of patience. Learning a new skill, mastering a craft, or achieving proficiency in a discipline takes time and consistent effort. The journey is often fraught with setbacks and challenges that test one's resolve."[1] Persistence, on the other hand, is the unwavering commitment to continue working toward a goal despite difficulties. Together, these qualities enable teams to navigate the complexities of long-term projects and initiatives.

To cultivate patience and persistence, teams should first set clear, long-term goals. These goals serve as a roadmap, providing direction and purpose. When team members understand the broader vision, they are more likely to stay committed, even when progress seems slow. Clear goals also help in breaking down the larger objective into smaller, manageable tasks. This approach not only makes the workload more digestible but also allows for regular assessment of progress and adjustments as needed. Celebrating milestones along the way is another critical strategy for maintaining motivation and a sense of progress. Each milestone represents a tangible achievement that brings the team closer to the ultimate goal. These celebrations can take various forms, from formal recognition ceremonies to informal team gatherings. The key is to acknowledge the hard work and perseverance that contributed to reaching these milestones, reinforcing the value of patience and persistence.

Resilience training can further equip team members with the necessary tools to handle setbacks and maintain a positive outlook. Techniques such as mindfulness and stress management are particularly effective in fostering a patient and persistent mindset. Mindfulness helps individuals stay present and focused, reducing anxiety about future uncertainties. Stress management techniques enable team members to cope with pressure and recover from setbacks more effectively. Together, these practices build a resilient workforce capable of sustaining long-term efforts. Moreover, fostering a culture that values patience and persistence is essential. Leaders play a pivotal role in this process. By modeling these behaviors and consistently reinforcing their importance, leaders can inspire their teams to adopt similar attitudes. Open communication is also crucial; when team members feel comfortable discussing challenges and setbacks, they are more likely to seek support and solutions collaboratively. This supportive environment enhances resilience and collective perseverance.

Encourage Focus on Incremental Progress Rather Than Immediate Results

Focusing on incremental progress helps teams stay motivated and reduces the pressure to achieve immediate success. This approach, which emphasizes continuous improvement and adaptability, can be a game-changer in maintaining team morale and achieving long-term goals. One specific paradigm involving this approach remains the agile methodology. As reported in *The Wall Street Journal*: "The agile craze has many potential benefits. There's no single definition of agile—it's a set of principles aimed at freeing teams from departmental silos and other bureaucracy so they can work more efficiently."[2] Within agile are many approaches, habits, and practices, one of which is the "breaking of big projects down into a series of smaller tasks, meeting daily to report progress and eliminate obstacles, and completing tasks in time periods called sprints."[3] Such a process allows team members to see their progress more clearly, which can be highly motivating and reinforce their commitment to the larger objective. The process of breaking down goals starts with identifying the end objective and then mapping out the steps required to achieve it. The steps used in this process are often defined as SMART: specific, measurable, achievable, realistic, and time-bound. It also provides a clear path forward, helping team members focus on what needs to be done now, rather than becoming paralyzed by the enormity of the end goal.

Regular check-ins and progress reviews are essential for keeping the team on track. These sessions provide opportunities to assess how well the team is progressing toward its goals and to make any necessary adjustments. By regularly reviewing progress, teams can identify potential issues early and address them before they become major obstacles. This iterative process of planning, acting, reviewing, and adjusting ensures continuous improvement and adaptability. Regular progress reviews also offer a platform for celebrating small wins, which can boost team morale and motivation. Recognizing and celebrating incremental achievements reinforces the value of each team member's contributions and fosters a positive team culture. This recognition can be as simple as verbal acknowledgment in meetings or more formal rewards and recognitions.

Utilizing data-driven feedback is another crucial component of focusing on incremental progress. Concrete evidence of progress helps reinforce the importance of small steps and provides clear indicators of success. Data-driven feedback can come from various sources, including performance metrics, project milestones, and individual contributions. This feedback not only shows how much progress has been made but also highlights areas that need improvement. By analyzing data, teams can make informed decisions about their strategies and workflows. One word of caution here, however, "Just because a decision is based on data doesn't mean it will always be correct. While the data might show a particular pattern or suggest a certain outcome, if the data collection process or interpretation is flawed, then any decision based on the data would be inaccurate."[4] As a result of this potential outcome, "the impact of every business decision should be regularly measured and monitored."[5]

Foster a Culture of Perseverance and Commitment Within the Team

A culture that values perseverance and commitment is essential for long-term success. Such an environment supports team members through challenges and maintains their dedication to collective goals. Leaders play a pivotal role in fostering a culture of perseverance and commitment. By exemplifying patience and a focus on long-term goals, leaders set a powerful example for their teams. Their actions and attitudes directly influence team dynamics and the overall work environment. When leaders consistently demonstrate perseverance, especially during challenging times, they inspire their teams to adopt similar behaviors. This modeling of resilience encourages team members to remain steadfast in their efforts and to view setbacks as temporary hurdles rather than insurmountable obstacles. As Robert David noted, leaders who demonstrate consistency can be relied upon. Therefore, "since a leader's actions naturally shape and inform the attitudes of those around them, a consistent leader can inspire consistent (and, by extension, persistent) teams. So, when a manager demonstrates an unwavering devotion to company success, their teammates are more likely to follow suit."[6]

A supportive team culture is built on open communication, where challenges and setbacks can be discussed without fear. Open communication allows team members to share their difficulties, seek advice, and collaborate on solutions. This transparency helps to demystify problems, making them more manageable and less intimidating. Moreover, when team members feel heard and understood, they are more likely to stay engaged and committed to their work. Encouraging open dialogue also fosters trust within the team, as members know they can rely on one another for support. This collective problem-solving approach not only strengthens the team's resilience but also enhances their ability to persevere through tough times. Recognition and rewards are crucial for reinforcing the values of perseverance and commitment. Acknowledging the efforts and achievements of team members, especially those who have demonstrated exceptional dedication, sends a strong message about what the organization values. This recognition can take various forms, such as verbal praise, formal awards, or even small gestures of appreciation. Recognizing perseverance encourages others to adopt similar behaviors. When team members see that their hard work and commitment are valued and rewarded, they are more likely to persevere through challenges. This positive reinforcement creates a cycle of motivation and dedication, where team members continually strive to meet and exceed expectations.

Building a supportive environment involves more than just open communication and recognition; it also includes providing the necessary resources and support systems. Leaders should ensure that team members have access to the tools and training they need to succeed. This might include professional development opportunities, mentorship programs, or even mental health resources to help manage stress and prevent burnout. A supportive environment also means creating a culture where failure is viewed as a learning opportunity rather than a defeat. By normalizing the idea that setbacks are part of the journey to success, leaders can help team members develop a growth mindset. This perspective encourages continuous learning and improvement, which are critical components of perseverance and long-term success.

Conclusion

In today's fast-paced world, where technology and information flow at unprecedented speeds, high-performing teams often face immense pressure to deliver quick results. This demand for rapid outcomes can create a culture of impatience, prioritizing short-term gains over sustainable, long-term success. However, to truly thrive, teams must balance this pressure with a strategic focus on lasting objectives. Patience and persistence are essential qualities for navigating setbacks and maintaining dedication to ambitious goals. By focusing on incremental progress rather than immediate results, teams can stay motivated and maintain momentum, with small, consistent steps accumulating into significant achievements over time. Fostering a culture of perseverance and commitment further supports this approach, creating an environment where dedication and resilience are nurtured and valued.

Self-Reflection Questions

1. How do I typically respond to the pressure of delivering quick results in my team or work environment?
2. Do I prioritize short-term gains over long-term success in my projects? Why or why not?
3. How can I better balance the immediate demands of my work with a strategic focus on lasting objectives?
4. In what ways do I cultivate patience and persistence in my professional life?
5. How do I navigate setbacks and maintain dedication to my ambitious goals?
6. What strategies do I use to stay motivated and maintain momentum when immediate results are not visible?
7. How do I break down large goals into smaller, manageable steps to achieve incremental progress?
8. How can I contribute to fostering a culture of perseverance and commitment within my team?
9. In what ways do I recognize and celebrate small, consistent achievements to reinforce ongoing effort and progress?
10. How do I create an environment that nurtures dedication and resilience among my team members or colleagues?

CHAPTER 9

Rely on Positive Uncertainty

Introduction

In today's fast-paced and ever-evolving world, high-performance teams confront uncertainty on an all too frequent basis. Uncertainty has become a constant companion in the landscape of business, technology, and society. In such an environment, the ability to embrace uncertainty and harness its potential becomes crucial for success. As Rebecca Zucker and Darin Rowell noted in "6 Strategies for Leading Through Uncertainty," their 2021 *Harvard Business Review* article "we must learn to acknowledge and embrace the discomfort of uncertainty as an expected and normal part of the learning process."[1] High-performance teams leverage positive uncertainty to shift their mindset, build team resilience, improve decision making, and enhance creativity.

Leverage Positive Uncertainty to Shift Your Mindset

For high-performance teams navigating uncertainty, a crucial shift in mindset is necessary. The traditional approach of strictly adhering to predefined plans and strategies often falls short in dynamic environments. Instead, teams must develop a mindset that embraces change, welcomes ambiguity, and views challenges as opportunities for growth. This fundamental shift enhances adaptability and fosters a culture of continuous learning and innovation, enabling teams to thrive even in uncertain conditions. In today's fast-paced world, the ability to pivot and adapt is essential. Recent research published in *The Wall Street Journal*, and conducted by the Drucker Institute, in conjunction with Korn Ferry, found that leaders of high-performing teams leverage positive uncertainty to shift their mindset. "The companies that score highest on the Drucker Institute gauge of corporate effectiveness are led by those who, according to Korn Ferry's psychometric assessments of thousands of individual executives, are tolerant of ambiguity and are adaptable."[2] This perspective highlights the need for teams to move away from rigid strategies and be prepared to adjust as circumstances evolve.

An adaptive mindset allows teams to quickly pivot strategies, which is particularly vital in industries marked by rapid technological advancements and shifting market dynamics. By embracing change, teams can stay ahead of the curve, continuously refining their approaches based on real-time feedback and emerging trends. This proactive stance is essential for maintaining a competitive edge and ensuring long-term success. Additionally, cultivating a mindset that sees challenges as growth opportunities transforms problem-solving approaches and fosters resilience. When teams reframe obstacles as learning experiences, they can drive innovation and improvement. This mindset shift empowers teams to tackle difficulties head-on, using them as catalysts for growth and development, ultimately driving progress in an ever-changing landscape. Such a process also allows high-performing teams to leverage positive uncertainty to build resilience.

Leverage Positive Uncertainty to Build Team Resilience

Building resilience is another critical trait for high-performance teams in uncertain times. Resilience equips teams with the ability to bounce back from setbacks, adapt to unforeseen circumstances, and persevere in the pursuit of their goals. In a volatile and unpredictable world, resilience acts as a shield against adversity, enabling teams to weather storms and emerge stronger than before. By cultivating resilience, teams develop the capacity to withstand challenges, maintain morale, and sustain high levels of performance even in the face of uncertainty. In today's fast-paced and ever-changing environment, resilience is not just a desirable trait but a necessity for survival and success. As organizations and teams face unprecedented disruptions—from economic fluctuations to global pandemics—the ability to recover quickly from setbacks is paramount. According to Mathew Lehnig, "resilience is the cornerstone of success, transforming challenges into opportunities and setbacks into breakthroughs." Leaders and high-performing teams learn how to "embrace resilience as their greatest asset, and then use it to propel them toward unprecedented growth and achievement."[3]

Resilience enables teams to adapt effectively to unforeseen challenges by remaining flexible, resourceful, and focused on their goals. When unexpected obstacles arise, resilient teams can reframe problems, explore alternative solutions, and adjust strategies to align with new realities. This adaptability is crucial for overcoming hurdles and maintaining progress, even under pressure. Moreover, resilience helps sustain high performance and morale during tough times, mitigating stress and burnout by fostering a supportive environment. Open communication, continuous learning, and recognition of resilience within the team are key strategies for building this essential quality. By prioritizing resilience, teams can maintain a proactive approach, reduce the impact of stress, and achieve long-term objectives. This endurance not only aids in recovery but also drives innovation and growth amidst challenges.

Improve Decision Making Through Positive Uncertainty

Improving decision making is crucial for high-performance teams operating in uncertain environments, where ambiguity and incomplete information complicate the process. In such situations, teams must hone their decision making skills to make informed and effective choices. Strategies such as scenario planning, data-driven analysis, and collaborative decision making help teams mitigate risks, seize opportunities, and navigate uncertainty with confidence. Scenario planning, in particular, is a powerful tool that allows teams to envision various future scenarios and develop strategies to address them. By preparing for multiple potential outcomes, teams can reduce the element of surprise and enhance their readiness to respond effectively. Data-driven analysis also plays a critical role by providing an objective foundation for decision making, helping teams uncover trends, identify patterns, and make more accurate decisions even with incomplete information.

Collaborative decision making is another essential strategy for high-performance teams in uncertain environments. By engaging team members at all levels in the decision making process, teams ensure that diverse perspectives and expertise are considered, leading to more balanced and well-rounded outcomes. Collaboration fosters a sense of ownership and commitment among team members, enhancing the overall quality of decisions and mitigating individual biases and errors. This approach leverages the collective intelligence of the team, ensuring more robust and effective choices. By drawing on the strengths and insights of all team members, collaborative decision making strengthens the team's ability to navigate uncertainty successfully. Together, these strategies not only improve decision making but also empower teams to thrive in dynamic and challenging environments. Moreover, as Rebecca Zucker and Darin Rowell noted, when the leader of a high-performing team, or one striving to be, reaches out for collaboration, one "exponentially expands their knowledge and perspective by cultivating and connecting with a network of peers and colleagues—each with their own set of experiences and perspectives."[4]

Use Positive Uncertainty to Enhance Creativity

Uncertainty inherently stimulates creativity by challenging the status quo and encouraging new ways of thinking. When faced with uncertain conditions, teams are compelled to move beyond their comfort zones and explore innovative solutions. According to an article in *Harvard Business Review*, "Creativity is often sparked by constraints and challenges that force us to rethink our assumptions and explore new possibilities."[5] This rethinking process is crucial in environments where traditional methods may no longer be effective. High-performance teams leverage this uncertainty as a driving force for creative problem-solving, pushing boundaries to uncover fresh perspectives and strategies.

Moreover, fostering a culture of experimentation is essential for nurturing creativity within teams, as it allows them to test new ideas, learn from failures, and refine their approaches. This iterative process not only enhances creative thinking but also builds resilience and adaptability, helping teams navigate uncertainty and drive innovation. By embracing a trial-and-error mindset, teams can continuously evolve and improve, leading to more innovative and effective solutions. In an environment where change is constant, creativity becomes a powerful tool for problem-solving and maintaining a competitive advantage. Creative teams are adept at identifying opportunities within challenges and leveraging them to differentiate their products or services. This ability to innovate and adapt swiftly is crucial for staying relevant and competitive in fast-paced industries. Ultimately, teams that prioritize creativity and experimentation are better positioned to thrive in dynamic environments.

Conclusion

Decades ago, Peter Drucker noted that executives could count on uncertainty more than almost anything else when leading an organization. "Uncertainty," as Drucker noted, "in the economy, society, politics—has become so great as to render futile, if not counterproductive, the kind of planning most companies still practice: forecasting based on probabilities."[6] Leaders still forecast based on probabilities but in 2025 and beyond, what the evidence overwhelming points to is that during the last two turbulent decades since Drucker's observation, high-performance teams, and their respective leaders, have learned to practice the valuable skill of relying on positive uncertainty to remain vital, vibrant, and relevant in a world of constant change and disruption.

Self-Reflection Questions

1. How do I typically respond to uncertainty in my work environment?
2. What strategies do I currently use to adapt to unexpected challenges?
3. How comfortable am I with embracing ambiguity and change in my decision making process?

4. In what ways can I shift my mindset to see challenges as opportunities for growth?
5. How do I foster resilience within my team to help them navigate uncertainty effectively?
6. What role does experimentation play in my approach to problem-solving and innovation?
7. How can I better leverage collaboration within my team to improve decision making?
8. In what ways do I encourage continuous learning and open communication to build a supportive team culture?
9. How do I currently use scenario planning and data-driven analysis to prepare for multiple future outcomes?
10. How can I further enhance creativity in my team by fostering a culture that embraces uncertainty and experimentation?

CHAPTER 10

Embrace VUCA – Inspired Dynamics

Introduction

In the modern business landscape, characterized by rapid change and disruption, high-performance teams must navigate an environment defined by VUCA. Embracing VUCA is crucial for fostering adaptability and ensuring sustained success. By understanding and leveraging VUCA dynamics, teams can enhance their resilience, innovation, and strategic decision making. Before delving into the specific reasons for embracing VUCA, it's essential to understand what each component represents:

- Volatility refers to the speed and unpredictability of change within an industry or market. For example, rapid advancements in technology, such as the introduction of 5G networks, can quickly alter market dynamics, forcing companies to adapt their strategies and operations almost overnight to stay competitive.
- Uncertainty involves the lack of predictability and clarity regarding future events. A prime example is the global COVID-19 pandemic, which created unprecedented uncertainty for businesses worldwide. Companies had to pivot to remote work, navigate supply chain disruptions, and manage fluctuating consumer demand without a clear understanding of how long the crisis would last or its long-term impacts.
- Complexity denotes the multitude of interconnected variables and the intricate nature of global systems. An example of complexity can be seen in the international automotive industry, where manufacturing a single vehicle involves coordinating

thousands of parts from multiple suppliers across different countries, each subject to their own regulations, economic conditions, and logistical challenges.

- Ambiguity highlights the lack of clarity about the meaning of an event or situation. For instance, when a new competitor enters the market with an innovative business model, it can create ambiguity for existing players. They must interpret whether this new model represents a sustainable shift in the industry or just a temporary trend and decide how to respond strategically amidst this lack of clear information.

By embracing and understanding these VUCA dynamics, high-performance teams can cultivate the necessary skills and mindset to thrive in such environments. They can enhance their resilience by preparing for and responding to rapid changes and unexpected challenges. Leveraging the uncertainty as a driver for innovation, teams can explore new ideas and approaches to stay ahead. Understanding complexity helps in making informed strategic decisions that consider the broader implications and interconnectedness of actions. Navigating ambiguity allows teams to remain flexible, continuously learn, and adapt strategies based on evolving interpretations and insights.

These elements collectively characterize the challenges that high-performance teams face today. Embracing VUCA is not merely about acknowledging these challenges but about developing strategies to thrive within them. As Ana Cernega and fellow researchers wrote: "This concept of VUCA has also been adopted in business, organizational management, and leadership, expanding into various areas."[1] Commenting on its impact, Cernega noted that "at its core, VUCA is a challenging view of reality. The VUCA concept has found its place in almost everything around us, from government policy to people's daily choices and decisions. It has been used to guide institutions and individuals to be less affected when faced with complex, unknown, and unseen phenomena."[2] To that end, high-performance teams that embrace the VUCA dynamics enhance their flexibility, rely on systems thinking, and build a culture of continuous learning find themselves more equipped to address "complex, unknown, and unseen phenomena."

Enhancing Flexibility

One of the primary reasons high-performance teams should embrace VUCA is to enhance their resilience and flexibility. In a VUCA environment, the ability to adapt quickly to changing conditions is paramount. Teams that cultivate resilience can better withstand shocks and recover from setbacks, while flexibility enables them to pivot strategies and seize emerging opportunities. As noted by a 2022 McKinsey study, "Nearly two-thirds of responding companies said that resilience is central to their organizations' strategic process—either as a top priority or to an important extent."[3] To thrive in a VUCA world, high-performance teams need to enhance their flexibility as they work on fostering a resilient mindset. This involves not only preparing for disruptions but also viewing them as opportunities for growth and innovation.

Resilience is built through continuous learning and development. High-performance teams must prioritize ongoing training and skill enhancement to stay ahead of industry trends. This approach ensures that team members are well-equipped to navigate volatility and uncertainty, making them more adaptable and robust in the face of challenges. Uncertainty, often seen as a hurdle, can be a powerful driver of innovation. When teams embrace uncertainty, they are more likely to experiment with new ideas and approaches. This experimental mindset fosters a culture of innovation where creative solutions can emerge. As Bambang Haryanto wrote, "Uncertainty pushes teams to think outside the box and explore unconventional solutions. It's in these moments of uncertainty that the most innovative ideas are born."[4] Haryanto's insight highlights the transformative potential of uncertainty. High-performance teams that embrace uncertainty are more likely to innovate and stay competitive in a rapidly changing market. Encouraging experimentation requires a supportive environment where failure is seen as a learning opportunity rather than a setback. Leaders play a crucial role in fostering this culture by promoting psychological safety and encouraging team members to take calculated risks. By doing so, they create an atmosphere where innovation can thrive.

Rely on Systems Thinking

High-performance teams rely on systems thinking to effectively navigate the VUCA dynamics because it allows them to see the bigger picture and understand how different elements within a system are interconnected. By recognizing the interdependencies within a system, teams can better anticipate the ripple effects of their decisions, making them more adept at managing complexity and uncertainty. Systems thinking encourages teams to look beyond immediate challenges and consider long-term impacts, which is crucial in volatile environments where change is constant. This holistic approach enables teams to identify leverage points where small changes can lead to significant improvements, helping them stay resilient and adaptive in the face of VUCA challenges.

Furthermore, systems thinking fosters a culture of collaboration and shared understanding within teams, which is essential for navigating ambiguity and making informed decisions. By viewing problems from multiple perspectives, teams can avoid siloed thinking and develop more innovative solutions that account for the complexities of their environment. This approach also helps teams align their actions with broader organizational goals, ensuring that their efforts contribute to overall success. Moreover, teams that adopt systems thinking are better equipped to respond to the unpredictability of VUCA environments by creating strategies that are both flexible and robust. This mindset not only enhances the team's ability to cope with VUCA dynamics but also empowers them to turn challenges into opportunities for growth and innovation.

Building a Culture of Continuous Learning

High-performance teams understand the importance of continuous learning as a critical strategy to thrive in VUCA environments. In a world where change is constant and often unpredictable, these teams prioritize learning to stay ahead of emerging trends and challenges. Continuous learning enables them to develop the agility and resilience needed to respond effectively to disruptions. By fostering a culture of learning, team members are encouraged to seek out new knowledge, embrace innovative approaches, and challenge existing assumptions. This proactive approach ensures that they are not merely reacting to changes but anticipating and shaping them. The ability to learn and adapt quickly becomes a competitive advantage, allowing high-performance teams to navigate the complexities of the VUCA world with confidence. Moreover, continuous learning helps these teams maintain a growth mindset, essential for ongoing improvement and long-term success.

In the context of VUCA dynamics, where uncertainty and complexity are prevalent, high-performance teams recognize that static knowledge is insufficient. They understand that to remain effective, they must continually update their skills and knowledge bases. This commitment to learning allows them to pivot swiftly in response to unforeseen challenges and opportunities. It also fosters a sense of collective intelligence within the team, where diverse perspectives and expertise are valued and integrated into decision making processes. By staying informed and adaptable, these teams are better equipped to manage ambiguity and reduce the risks associated with volatility. Furthermore, continuous learning reinforces collaboration, as team members share insights and lessons learned, enhancing overall team performance. In essence, the commitment to continuous learning enables high-performance teams to remain resilient, innovative, and effective in the face of the ever-changing demands of the VUCA landscape. As Dede Henley wrote in *Forbes*: "The best leaders I've coached can look at circumstances through a variety of lenses, shifting perspectives with ease. That enables them to keep an open mind and be influenced by those who hold a different perspective. They are curious, open learners."[5]

Conclusion

In conclusion, high-performance teams operating in today's VUCA world must embrace volatility, uncertainty, complexity, and ambiguity as fundamental elements that shape their success. The ability to adapt quickly and maintain resilience is paramount, enabling teams to turn disruptions into opportunities for growth and innovation. By leveraging systems thinking, teams can understand the interconnectedness of challenges and make more informed, strategic decisions. This holistic approach not only enhances problem-solving but also fosters collaboration, ensuring that diverse perspectives are considered in decision-making processes. Furthermore, continuous learning serves as a cornerstone for teams to stay ahead of evolving trends and maintain agility in the face of uncertainty. As teams cultivate a growth mindset, they become more innovative and better equipped to handle the complexities of a rapidly changing environment. With the right leadership, organizational support, and a culture of psychological safety, teams can thrive in the midst of ambiguity. Ultimately, embracing VUCA dynamics allows high-performance teams to remain flexible, innovative, and resilient, ensuring sustained success in an unpredictable world.

Self-Reflection Questions

1. How well do I understand the concepts of VUCA, and how they apply to my team's work environment?

2. In what ways has my team responded to rapid changes in our industry or market, and how did our approach reflect our understanding of VUCA dynamics?

3. How can I improve my team's adaptability and resilience in the face of unpredictable and volatile situations?

4. How does my team currently handle uncertainty, and what steps can we take to leverage it as a driver of innovation rather than a source of stress?

5. What strategies can I implement to better manage the complexity in our work, ensuring that we consider the broader implications of our decisions?

6. How does my team currently approach ambiguous situations, and what can we do to improve our ability to interpret and respond to unclear events?

7. How do I foster a culture of continuous learning within my team, and how does this contribute to our success in a VUCA environment?

8. In what ways can I encourage systems thinking within my team to better navigate the interconnected challenges we face in our industry?

9. How well do I support experimentation and calculated risk-taking within my team, and how does this impact our ability to innovate and adapt?

10. How can I enhance collaboration and the sharing of diverse perspectives in my team to better tackle the complexities and uncertainties of our work environment?

CHAPTER 11

Have a Bias Toward Action

Introduction

High-performing teams are distinguished by their ability to act decisively and effectively in challenging situations. Having a bias toward action is a cognitive bias important for personal and professional growth. This essential skill of having a bias towards action is simply not about moving fast for the sake of it. Having a bias towards action specifically refers to recognizing the need to reduce the time between idea conception and value creation while maintaining quality and alignment with long-term goals. For example, having a bias toward action is one of the key leadership principles of Amazon that states: "Speed matters in business. Many decisions and actions are reversible and do not need extensive study. We value calculated risk taking."[1] This bias toward action manifests in three critical components: promoting a culture of experimentation and rapid prototyping, encouraging initiative and decisiveness in problem-solving, and fostering a mindset of learning through action and iteration. These components are essential for driving innovation, responsiveness, and continuous improvement within teams.

Promoting a Culture of Experimentation and Rapid Prototyping

Promoting a culture of experimentation and rapid prototyping is essential for high-performing teams, as it encourages them to test ideas quickly, learn from failures, and iterate on solutions, fostering an innovative environment. This approach allows teams to validate ideas and pivot when necessary, maintaining agility in dynamic markets. By moving beyond traditional frameworks and embracing a more adaptive problem-solving process, teams create a continuous feedback loop where ideas are constantly tested, refined, and improved. This iterative method is crucial for identifying viable solutions early and discarding less promising ones before significant resources are invested, ultimately reducing the fear of failure and encouraging calculated risks that drive innovation.

A culture of experimentation empowers teams to explore creative solutions without the fear of failure, which is a key driver of innovation. When team members feel safe to experiment, they are more likely to share bold ideas and collaborate effectively, knowing that even if an experiment fails, it is seen as a learning opportunity rather than a setback. This aligns with agile methodologies, which prioritize responsiveness to change and incremental progress, allowing teams to deliver functional iterations of products quickly and efficiently. Companies such as Google and Amazon have built their success on continuous experimentation and rapid prototyping, demonstrating how this approach can lead to groundbreaking innovations that meet user needs and market demands. As Jerry Wind, Lauder Professor and professor of marketing at the Wharton School of the University of Pennsylvania noted, "Experimentation is great because, No. 1, it's the only way to really find out if there's a link between actions and results; No. 2, it forces people to measure; No. 3, it leads to better decisions; and No. 4, it creates a culture of innovation."[2]

Encouraging Initiative and Decisiveness in Problem-Solving

Encouraging initiative and decisiveness in problem-solving is a hallmark of high-performing teams, enabling them to address issues swiftly without waiting for approval from higher-ups. This approach not only speeds up the problem-solving process but also fosters a sense of ownership and accountability among team members. When teams are empowered to make decisions, they become more agile and responsive, better equipped to navigate the complexities of today's business environment. Delegating decision-making authority taps into the diverse perspectives and expertise within the team, leading to more innovative and effective solutions while cultivating a culture of trust and respect where employees feel valued and confident in their roles.

Moreover, decisiveness in problem-solving significantly enhances operational efficiency by reducing downtime and enabling teams to respond effectively to unforeseen challenges. Swift decision-making mitigates risks and prevents minor issues from escalating into major problems, ensuring the continuity and efficiency of operations. Empowering teams with decision-making capabilities also improves project outcomes, as studies show that teams with high decision-making authority are more likely to complete projects on time and within budget. For example, when a manager brings people "into the conversation with different disciplinary and cultural backgrounds, the team often enhances its creativity and gains a fresh perspective on the task or problem at hand."[3] Additionally, fostering a culture of decisiveness boosts employee engagement and retention, as employees who feel empowered to make decisions are more motivated, committed, and less likely to leave the organization. This culture of empowerment and trust ultimately drives sustained success and enhances overall organizational performance.

Fostering a Mindset of Learning Through Action and Iteration

Fostering a mindset of learning through action and iteration is crucial for continuous improvement in high-performing teams. These teams view mistakes as valuable learning opportunities, constantly refining their processes based on real-world feedback. This iterative approach ensures ongoing improvement and adaptability to new information, particularly within agile environments where breaking down projects into manageable tasks is key. By completing tasks in short cycles or sprints, teams can regularly assess their performance, identify areas for improvement, and quickly respond to changes and unforeseen challenges, maintaining high levels of quality and efficiency.

Continuous improvement through iterative learning not only enhances team performance but also provides a competitive edge by enabling teams to evolve their skills and strategies. Organizations that support this approach by providing the necessary tools, training, and a culture of knowledge sharing empower their teams to approach tasks with confidence and creativity. Practical examples, such as Toyota's Kaizen philosophy, demonstrate the effectiveness of small, incremental changes leading to significant improvements over time. This mindset is particularly vital in fast-paced sectors such as technology and software development, where companies such as Google and Amazon use iterative processes to quickly release and refine products, staying ahead in rapidly changing markets. Research by McKinsey concluded: "Core to a continuous improvement mindset is the belief that a steady stream of improvements, diligently executed, will have transformational results."[4] In a world marked by constant disruption, having transformational results is paramount for an organization to remain vital, vibrant, and relevant.

Conclusion

In conclusion, high-performing teams thrive by embracing a bias toward action, which is pivotal for navigating the challenges of today's fast-paced business environment. This mindset is evident in their approach to experimentation, decisiveness in problem-solving, and a commitment to continuous learning and iteration. By fostering a culture where calculated risks are encouraged, these teams can innovate rapidly, adapt to new information, and maintain agility in dynamic markets. Empowering team members to take initiative and make decisions not only enhances operational efficiency but also cultivates a sense of ownership and accountability, driving sustained success. Additionally, the iterative learning process allows teams to refine their strategies continuously, staying ahead of competition and effectively managing change. Organizations that support these principles through tools, training, and a culture of trust position themselves to achieve transformational results. Ultimately, the combination of these practices ensures that high-performing teams remain resilient, innovative, and well-equipped to meet the demands of an ever-evolving marketplace.

Self-Reflection Questions

Here are 10 self-reflection questions based on the provided text:

1. How do I currently approach decision-making in challenging situations, and do I tend to favor action or inaction?
2. What steps can I take to embrace calculated risks in both my personal and professional lives?
3. How comfortable am I with experimenting and rapidly prototyping new ideas, and how can I improve in this area?
4. In what ways do I encourage or hinder a culture of experimentation within my team or organization?
5. How can I better promote initiative and decisiveness in problem-solving within my team?
6. When faced with an unexpected challenge, how quickly do I typically respond, and what strategies could enhance my responsiveness?
7. How do I view mistakes—do I see them as failures or opportunities for learning and improvement?
8. What practices can I adopt to foster a mindset of continuous improvement through iterative learning?
9. How well do I integrate feedback loops into my work processes, and how can I use feedback more effectively?
10. What tools or resources could I leverage to support a culture of trust, empowerment, and innovation within my team or organization?

CHAPTER 12

Assess How You Make Decisions

Introduction

Decision-making plays a crucial role in a manager's daily responsibilities. Whether reshuffling the department's budget, delegating tasks, or implementing a new strategy, each decision a manager makes directly influences the organization's success. However, navigating the decision-making process often presents challenges. A survey by management consulting firm McKinsey revealed that only 28 percent of executives praised the quality of their company's strategic decisions, while 60 percent acknowledged that poor decisions occur almost as often as good ones.[1] To help teams become high-performing, managers and leaders understand the value of rigorously assessing their decision-making processes to ensure that they remain competitive and effective. Three such reasons why high-performing teams assess their decision-making process involves avoiding groupthink, leveraging cognitive diversity, and promoting critical thinking.

Avoiding Groupthink

Groupthink presents a substantial challenge to effective decision-making, often creating an environment where the desire for harmony and consensus takes precedence over critical evaluation. In such situations, team members may suppress their individual thoughts and concerns, prioritizing group cohesion over the exploration of diverse viewpoints. This dynamic can lead to a narrowing of perspectives, where alternative ideas and potential risks are ignored, ultimately resulting in suboptimal decisions. In his 1972 study *Victims of Groupthink: A Psychological Study of Foreign-Policy Decisions and Fiascoes,* social psychologist Irving Janis identified groupthink as a common issue in cohesive groups, emphasizing that the drive for unanimity can override the motivation to appraise all options critically. Recognizing this risk, high-performing teams adopt strategies to counteract groupthink by fostering an atmosphere of open dialogue and encouraging dissenting opinions. This proactive approach allows for the consideration of a wider array of perspectives, ensuring that all potential solutions are thoroughly evaluated. By doing so, these teams can mitigate the risks associated with conformity and make decisions that are both well-informed and balanced.

The practice of encouraging diverse viewpoints not only enhances decision-making but also strengthens the team's overall problem-solving capabilities. When dissenting opinions are welcomed, team members feel empowered to share their unique insights and challenge prevailing assumptions. This creates a more dynamic and innovative decision-making process, where ideas are tested against a variety of perspectives before a final decision is reached. As noted by Irving Janis, "The more amiability and esprit de corps among the members of a policy-making in-group, the greater the danger that independent critical thinking will be replaced by groupthink."[2] To prevent this, successful teams implement mechanisms such as structured debates, devil's advocacy, and anonymous feedback channels, which help to surface concerns that might otherwise go unvoiced. By actively seeking out and addressing potential blind spots, these teams can avoid the pitfalls of groupthink and arrive at decisions that are not only more robust but also more likely to lead to positive outcomes for the organization.

Leveraging Cognitive Diversity

Cognitive diversity, the inclusion of team members with varied thinking styles and perspectives, serves as a critical asset for high-performing teams. This diversity enriches the decision-making process by bringing together individuals who approach problems from different angles, allowing the team to challenge conventional thinking and explore a broader spectrum of possibilities. By incorporating diverse viewpoints, teams can avoid the pitfalls of homogenous thinking, which often leads to overlooked opportunities and underestimated risks. Research supports the value of cognitive diversity, with a study by *Harvard Business Review* indicating that teams with diverse members solve problems faster than teams composed of similar individuals.[3] High-performing teams understand this advantage and strategically select members with diverse backgrounds, experiences, and expertise. This deliberate inclusion fosters an environment where creative solutions can emerge, as each team member contributes unique insights and challenges prevailing assumptions. As a result, the decision-making process becomes more dynamic, thorough, and likely to lead to innovative outcomes that are well-informed and balanced.

Moreover, cognitive diversity within teams enhances the ability to identify and mitigate risks that might otherwise go unnoticed. When team members with different perspectives collaborate, they are more likely to anticipate potential challenges and address them proactively. This foresight is particularly valuable in complex decision-making scenarios, where the stakes are high and the consequences of overlooking critical details can be significant. A 2019 study published in the *Frontiers in Psychology* found "having a moderate amount of cognitive style diversity facilitates such team ability since having too little is unlikely to provide teams with the cognitive capacity and flexibility to tackle tasks that require different ways of encoding and processing information, while having too much is likely to disrupt coordination in teams."[4] By leveraging the varied expertise and experiences of team members, high-performing teams can engage in comprehensive risk analysis, ensuring that all potential outcomes are considered. This approach not only reduces the likelihood of negative surprises but also strengthens the overall quality of decisions made. As Scott Page, author of *The Diversity Bonus,* notes, "Diverse groups of people bring to organizations more and different ways of seeing a problem and, thus, faster/better ways of solving it."[5] In this way, cognitive diversity becomes a vital component of successful team dynamics, driving innovation and enhancing the robustness of decisions.

Promoting Critical Thinking

Critical thinking plays a pivotal role in effective decision-making within teams, serving as the foundation for sound, innovative choices. High-performing teams recognize the importance of cultivating a culture that emphasizes rigorous analysis and evidence-based decision-making. By fostering an environment where team members are encouraged to question assumptions, evaluate the merits of various options, and consider the potential consequences of their decisions, these teams ensure that their choices are well-informed and strategically aligned with their objectives. This emphasis on critical thinking enables teams to navigate the complexities of decision-making with greater precision, reducing the likelihood of costly errors or missed opportunities. This approach not only enhances the quality of decisions made but also promotes a deeper understanding of the issues at hand, leading to more innovative and sustainable solutions. As a result, teams that prioritize critical thinking are better equipped to adapt to changing circumstances and maintain their competitive edge. As *Forbes* noted in an April 28, 2024 article, critical thinking is one of the top soft skills employers continue to look for in candidates and work to develop in employees.[6]

In addition to driving innovation and sound decision-making, critical thinking helps teams to identify and mitigate biases that can otherwise compromise the quality of their choices. Cognitive biases, such as confirmation bias or groupthink, often lead teams to make decisions based on incomplete or skewed information, potentially undermining their effectiveness. However, by promoting critical thinking, teams can create an environment where biases are recognized and addressed, leading to more objective and balanced decision-making. A study in the *Harvard Business Review* emphasizes the importance of critical thinking in avoiding these pitfalls, noting that teams with strong critical thinking skills are more adept at aligning their decisions with the company's long-term goals. This alignment ensures that the decisions made not only address immediate challenges but also support the organization's broader strategic objectives. In a culture that values critical thinking, teams are more likely to engage in reflective practices, continuously assessing and refining their decision-making processes to achieve sustained success. As Peter Facione, a leading expert in critical thinking, asserts, "Critical thinking is essential as a tool of inquiry. It helps us acquire knowledge, improve our theories, and strengthen arguments."[7] By embedding critical thinking into their decision-making frameworks, high-performing teams enhance their ability to make choices that drive both immediate and long-term success.

Conclusion

Decision-making stands as a cornerstone of effective management, directly influencing an organization's success and sustainability. High-performing teams understand that their ability to make sound decisions hinges on avoiding groupthink, leveraging cognitive diversity, and promoting critical thinking. By fostering open dialogue, embracing diverse perspectives, and rigorously analyzing options, these teams are equipped to navigate complex challenges and identify innovative solutions. They prioritize a decision-making process that is both inclusive and reflective, ensuring that all potential risks and benefits are thoroughly evaluated. This comprehensive approach not only enhances the quality of decisions but also aligns them with the organization's long-term goals. As a result, high-performing teams are better positioned to adapt to changing circumstances, drive innovation, and achieve sustained success. Ultimately, their commitment to refining decision-making processes serves as a key factor in maintaining a competitive edge in today's dynamic business environment.

Self-Reflection Questions

1. How do I currently approach decision-making in my team or organization, and what areas could benefit from improvement?
2. What steps do I take to ensure that my team avoids groupthink, and how can I further encourage open dialogue and dissenting opinions?

3. In what ways do I leverage cognitive diversity within my team to enhance decision-making, and how can I better include diverse perspectives?

4. How often do I encourage critical thinking among my team members, and what strategies could I implement to foster a culture of rigorous analysis?

5. How do I balance the need for consensus with the importance of thoroughly evaluating all options and potential risks?

6. What mechanisms do I have in place to identify and mitigate biases in my team's decision-making process?

7. How effectively does my team's decision-making process align with our organization's long-term goals, and where might there be misalignment?

8. In what ways can I improve the inclusiveness and reflectiveness of our decision-making process to ensure that all voices are heard and considered?

9. How do I encourage my team to adapt to changing circumstances, and how does this flexibility impact our ability to innovate and succeed?

10. What can I do to continuously refine and improve our decision-making processes to maintain a competitive edge in our industry?

CHAPTER 13

Respond With Intention and Care

Introduction

High-performing teams excel because they cultivate the crucial skill of responding with intention and care. This practice builds trust, enhances communication, and creates a culture of respect. When team members respond thoughtfully, they align their words with their goals and values, minimizing misunderstandings. This approach also demonstrates an appreciation for different perspectives, which fosters collaboration and sparks innovation. By mastering this skill, teams navigate conflicts more effectively, transforming challenges into growth opportunities. Over time, this habit strengthens the team culture, ensuring that everyone feels heard and valued. Unfortunately, this essential skill is lacking in many corporations, government agencies, and not-for-profit organizations since many, according to David R. Kolzow, "tend to be over-managed and underled."[1] By responding with intention, members of high-performing teams demonstrate commitment to the team's success, leading to better outcomes and a more cohesive working environment.

Demonstrate Commitment to Team's Success

High-performing teams consistently exhibit the essential skill of responding with intention and care, a practice that underpins their success. When team members communicate thoughtfully, they ensure that their responses are purposeful and aligned with the team's objectives. This intentional approach prevents hasty reactions and reduces the likelihood of misunderstandings, allowing the team to maintain clarity and focus. Responding with care also reflects a deep respect for colleagues' ideas and contributions, fostering an environment where every voice feels valued. By prioritizing this mindful communication, teams build stronger relationships, which, in turn, enhances collaboration. In this way, team members support one another, knowing their input will be met with consideration rather than dismissal. The practice of responding with intention and care becomes a cornerstone of trust, enabling the team to work more cohesively and effectively. As a result, the team moves forward with a united sense of purpose, consistently achieving high standards of performance.

This skill also directly demonstrates a commitment to the team's success. When members respond with intention and care, they show that they prioritize the team's goals over personal agendas, which reinforces a collective mindset. Such behavior signals to others that every decision and action is made with the team's best interest in mind, strengthening the shared commitment to success. Moreover, this thoughtful approach empowers team members to navigate challenges and conflicts constructively, turning potential setbacks into opportunities for learning and growth. As they engage in meaningful dialogue, the team develops resilience, adapting to changes and overcoming obstacles more effectively. By fostering an atmosphere where intentional communication is the norm, teams not only enhance their own performance but also contribute to the overall success of the organization. Ultimately, responding with intention and care reflects a deep-rooted dedication to the team's long-term achievements, ensuring sustained success in a competitive environment.

Lead to Better Outcomes

High-performing teams excel by mastering the essential skill of responding with intention and care, a practice that directly leads to better outcomes. When team members respond thoughtfully, they ensure that their words and actions align with the team's goals, which minimizes confusion and keeps everyone focused. This intentional communication prevents misunderstandings and allows the team to operate more efficiently, as everyone has a clear understanding of expectations and objectives. By responding with care, team members also demonstrate respect for each other's ideas and contributions, creating an environment where everyone feels valued. This respect fosters a collaborative atmosphere, encouraging open dialogue and the sharing of diverse perspectives, which often leads to more innovative solutions. As a result, the team can tackle challenges more effectively, leveraging the collective wisdom of its members. Intentional and caring responses build trust within the team, which enhances cooperation and ensures that the team functions as a cohesive unit. This cohesion is key to achieving consistently high performance and better outcomes.

Moreover, responding with intention and care positively influences the decision-making process within high-performing teams. When team members take the time to consider the impact of their responses, they contribute to more thoughtful and strategic decisions that align with the team's long-term goals. This careful consideration reduces the likelihood of rushed or poorly informed choices, which can derail progress and lead to suboptimal results. Additionally, when team members feel heard and respected, they are more likely to engage fully and contribute their best ideas, knowing that their input will be taken seriously. This leads to a more inclusive decision-making process where the best ideas rise to the top, driving better outcomes. Furthermore, the habit of responding with intention and care fosters a culture of accountability, as team members understand the importance of their role in the team's success. Over time, this leads to a continuous cycle of improvement, where the team consistently refines its processes and strategies. In this way, the skill of responding with intention and care not only enhances immediate outcomes but also contributes to the team's sustained success.

Develop a More Cohesive Working Environment

High-performing teams cultivate the essential skill of responding with intention and care, which plays a crucial role in developing a more cohesive working environment. When team members communicate thoughtfully, they demonstrate a deep respect for one another, which builds trust and fosters mutual understanding. This intentional approach to communication ensures that everyone feels heard and valued, reducing the likelihood of conflicts and misunderstandings.

As a result, team members are more likely to collaborate effectively, knowing that their contributions are respected and appreciated. This sense of respect and understanding strengthens the bonds within the team, leading to a more harmonious and united group. Additionally, by responding with care, team members show empathy and consideration for each other's perspectives, which further enhances the sense of unity. Over time, this creates a positive and supportive atmosphere where individuals are motivated to work together toward common goals. A cohesive working environment, built on the foundation of intentional and caring communication, allows the team to function more smoothly and efficiently.

This cohesive environment, fostered by intentional and caring responses, also enhances the team's ability to navigate challenges together. When team members feel connected and supported, they are more likely to approach problems with a collaborative mindset, seeking solutions that benefit the entire group rather than just themselves. This collective approach to problem-solving not only leads to better outcomes but also reinforces the team's unity, as they work together to overcome obstacles. Furthermore, a cohesive team environment encourages open and honest communication, where individuals feel safe to express their ideas and concerns without fear of judgment. This openness leads to more creative and effective solutions, as the team can tap into the full range of its members' talents and perspectives. As the team continues to respond with intention and care, this cycle of collaboration and support becomes ingrained in the team's culture. The result is a strong, cohesive working environment where everyone is aligned and committed to achieving shared goals. In such an environment, the team is not only more effective but also more resilient, able to adapt and thrive in the face of challenges.

Conclusion

In a January 2024 *Harvard Business Review* article, Amy Webb noted, "We are in the most challenging operating environment I've seen in 20 years, and this moment demands a new mindset."[2] The world in 2025 and for the immediate near future requires leaders to understand the value and utility of responding with intention and care as employees struggle to deal with complexity and uncertainty. As leaders, managers, and employees alike work toward developing a new mindset for today's VUCA marketplace, they would serve themselves well by remembering to practice the essential skill of responding with intention and care since doing so demonstrates a commitment to the team's success, leads to better outcomes and a forms a more cohesive working environment.

Self-Reflection Questions

1. How do I currently demonstrate intention and care in my responses within my team?
2. In what ways do my communication habits build or hinder trust and mutual understanding among my team members?
3. How well do my words and actions align with the team's goals and values during interactions?
4. Do I take the time to thoughtfully consider the perspectives of others before responding, and how does this influence our collaboration?
5. How effective am I in navigating conflicts within the team by using intentional and caring communication?
6. What specific actions can I take to ensure that every team member feels heard and valued in our discussions?
7. How does my approach to responding contribute to or detract from the team's cohesion and overall working environment?
8. In what ways can I improve my ability to prioritize the team's goals over personal agendas in my communication?
9. How do my responses influence the decision-making process within the team, and what can I do to enhance this impact?
10. What steps can I take to foster a culture of intentional and caring communication that leads to better outcomes and a more resilient team environment?

CHAPTER 14

Allow Yourself to Be Vulnerable

Introduction

The last two decades have witnessed new research on the role vulnerability has for both leaders and high-performing teams. As Patrick Lencioni wrote in a June 22, 2010, *Wall Street Journal* article, when discussing leadership or teamwork "there is no more powerful attribute than the ability to be genuinely honest about one's weaknesses, mistakes, and needs for help. Nothing inspires trust in another human being like vulnerability—there is just something immensely attractive and inspiring about humility and graciousness."[1] High-performance teams understand that allowing vulnerability fosters trust, which serves as the foundation for collaboration. Additionally, vulnerability encourages creativity and innovation; thus, when individuals feel free to share unconventional ideas or admit that they don't have all the answers, it creates an environment where experimentation thrives. Lastly, embracing vulnerability within a team promotes resilience. When people openly share challenges or failures, the team can collectively address and overcome obstacles. Fostering trust, encouraging creativity, and promoting resilience are three of the many reasons why high-performing teams invite vulnerability as a key characteristic of members.

Fostering Trust

High-performing teams leverage vulnerability as a cornerstone for building trust by creating a safe environment where team members feel comfortable expressing their authentic selves. When individuals share their uncertainties, challenges, or mistakes, they signal that they trust their colleagues to respond with empathy rather than judgment. This openness removes barriers to genuine communication, allowing team members to understand each other's strengths, weaknesses, and concerns. By acknowledging their own vulnerabilities, leaders set the tone for the entire team, demonstrating that asking for help or admitting a mistake is not a sign of weakness but a pathway to growth. This mutual trust enables the team to collaborate more effectively, as members feel assured that their contributions will be valued, even if they occasionally fall short. Over time, this culture of openness strengthens the bonds between team members, leading to deeper relationships and a more cohesive team dynamic. Trust, once established through shared vulnerability, becomes self-reinforcing, allowing the team to tackle challenges with greater unity and confidence.

Moreover, high-performing teams use vulnerability to enhance problem-solving and decision-making processes. When team members feel safe enough to express doubts or admit when they lack knowledge, it invites a broader range of perspectives and insights into discussions. This openness ensures that the team considers all possibilities and doesn't overlook potential pitfalls due to fear of criticism or rejection. By fostering a culture where vulnerability is embraced, the team can address issues more comprehensively, as everyone feels empowered to contribute without the fear of being judged. This inclusivity not only improves the quality of decisions but also increases the commitment of team members to the chosen course of action, as they feel genuinely heard and respected. Additionally, when challenges arise, the established trust allows the team to navigate conflicts more constructively, focusing on solutions rather than assigning blame. In this way, vulnerability not only builds trust but also drives the team's ability to innovate and adapt, ensuring sustained high performance.

Encouraging Creativity and Innovation

High-performing teams leverage vulnerability to encourage creativity by fostering an environment where team members feel safe to share unconventional ideas without fear of judgment. When individuals know that their suggestions, no matter how outlandish, will be met with open-mindedness rather than criticism, they become more willing to take creative risks. This openness is crucial for innovation, as ground-breaking ideas often emerge from thinking outside traditional boundaries. By embracing vulnerability, teams can explore a wider range of possibilities, leading to more innovative solutions. The willingness to express uncertainty or admit gaps in knowledge also plays a key role, as it encourages collaborative brainstorming where diverse perspectives can combine to generate novel concepts. Leaders in these teams model vulnerability by admitting when they don't have all the answers, signaling that the team should prioritize creativity over perfection. This approach transforms the fear of failure into an opportunity for learning and growth, further fueling the team's creative potential.

Furthermore, vulnerability in high-performing teams drives continuous innovation by promoting a culture of experimentation and learning. When team members feel secure enough to try new approaches and potentially fail, they open the door to iterative improvements and breakthroughs. This culture of experimentation relies on the team's collective ability to share both successes and failures openly, viewing them as valuable learning experiences rather than setbacks. By normalizing the sharing of vulnerabilities, teams reduce the stigma around failure, making it easier to pivot and adapt when things don't go as planned. This dynamic environment, where every idea is worth exploring and every outcome provides insight, fosters a cycle of innovation that propels the team forward. Additionally, the trust built through shared vulnerability enhances collaboration, as team members feel more comfortable building on each other's ideas, leading to more refined and innovative outcomes. In this way, vulnerability not only sparks creativity but also sustains it, ensuring that the team remains at the forefront of innovation.

Promoting Resilience

High-performing teams leverage vulnerability to promote resilience by fostering a culture where challenges and setbacks are openly discussed rather than hidden. When team members feel safe admitting their struggles or failures, it creates an environment where problems are addressed collectively rather than shouldered individually. This openness allows the team to quickly identify issues and mobilize resources to overcome them, preventing small challenges from escalating into larger crises. By encouraging vulnerability, teams ensure that no one suffers in silence, which not only helps solve problems faster but also strengthens the sense of unity and support within the team. Leaders play a crucial role by modeling vulnerability, sharing their own difficulties, and showing that resilience is built through mutual support rather than individual toughness. This collective approach to problem-solving enables the team to bounce back from setbacks more effectively, as everyone is invested in finding solutions. The shared experience of overcoming adversity together strengthens the bonds between team members, making the team more cohesive and resilient in the face of future challenges.

Vulnerability in high-performing teams also helps foster resilience by promoting a growth mindset, where mistakes and failures are viewed as opportunities for learning and improvement. When team members feel comfortable acknowledging their vulnerabilities, they are more likely to seek feedback, learn from their experiences, and apply those lessons to future challenges. This continuous learning process helps the team adapt to changing circumstances, turning potential obstacles into stepping stones for growth. The culture of vulnerability also reduces the fear of failure, encouraging team members to take calculated risks, knowing that they have the support of their colleagues regardless of the outcome. This approach not only builds individual resilience but also enhances the team's collective ability to navigate uncertainty and change. As a result, the team becomes more agile, able to pivot and adjust strategies as needed, which is essential for maintaining high performance in dynamic environments. Ultimately, by embracing vulnerability, high-performing teams create a resilient culture that thrives on learning, adaptation, and mutual support. As Brent Gleeson, an officer in charge of one of the most clandestine training organizations in Naval Special Warfare wrote in *Forbes*, "When you are vulnerable, you tend to accept that uncertainty is normal, risk is inevitable, and your emotional exposure process is viewed from a different lens. It is easier to admit that you don't know everything. It opens a path to personal acceptance, accelerated growth, emotional independence, and personal empowerment."[2]

Conclusion

Over the past two decades, research has increasingly highlighted the importance of vulnerability in both leadership and high-performing teams. Vulnerability fosters trust, allowing team members to feel safe sharing their weaknesses, mistakes, and uncertainties, which strengthens collaboration. This openness also encourages creativity, as individuals feel free to propose unconventional ideas and take risks, leading to innovative solutions. Additionally, a culture of vulnerability promotes resilience by enabling teams to address challenges collectively, view failures as learning opportunities, and adapt to changing circumstances. Leaders play a crucial role by modeling vulnerability, setting the tone for a supportive and growth-oriented environment. This approach reduces the fear of failure, enhances problem-solving, and helps teams navigate conflicts constructively. Ultimately, by embracing vulnerability, high-performing teams build trust, encourage creativity, and develop resilience, ensuring sustained success and adaptability in dynamic environments.

Self-Reflection Questions

1. How comfortable am I with expressing my own vulnerabilities, such as admitting mistakes or asking for help in a team setting?
2. In what ways do I foster an environment of trust within my team, where others feel safe to be vulnerable?
3. How do I respond when a team member shares a challenge or failure? Do I offer empathy and support, or do I tend to judge?
4. What actions can I take to encourage more open and honest communication within my team?
5. How do I balance the need for creativity with the fear of failure in my decision-making processes?

6. When faced with uncertainty or a lack of knowledge, how willing am I to admit it and seek input from others?

7. How do I view and handle failures within my team? Do I see them as opportunities for learning and growth?

8. In what ways do I model vulnerability as a leader, and how does this impact the team's culture?

9. How do I ensure that all team members feel their contributions are valued, even if their ideas are unconventional or risky?

10. How resilient is my team when facing setbacks, and what role does vulnerability play in helping us recover and adapt?

CHAPTER 15

Remain Open to Serendipity

Introduction

Over the years, companies such as Google, Pixar, and Zappos have incorporated the role of serendipitous communication among employees into their office space designs. Evidence from research studies suggests that those colleagues who work in close proximity to each other often experience an increase in collaboration. For example, "researchers at the University of Michigan studying 172 research scientists recently found that when the scientists shared the same buildings and overlapped in their daily workplace walking patterns—moving between lab space, office space, and the nearest bathroom and elevator—they were significantly more likely to collaborate. For every 100 feet of "zonal overlap," collaborations increased by up to 20 percent."[1] High-performing teams remain open to serendipity because it allows them to discover unexpected opportunities, fosters a culture of curiosity, and enhances a culture of collaboration across the organization.

Discover Unexpected Opportunities

High-performing teams should remain open to practicing serendipity because it allows them to discover unexpected opportunities that can lead to innovation and growth. In today's dynamic and rapidly changing environment, teams that embrace the unpredictable are better equipped to adapt quickly to new situations and challenges. This adaptability is crucial in a landscape where technological advances and market conditions can shift dramatically overnight. By fostering a mindset that values the unexpected, teams are more likely to encounter novel ideas and solutions that might not arise through conventional planning and execution. Serendipity encourages a proactive approach to learning and problem-solving, making it easier for teams to pivot when necessary. This ability to seize unforeseen opportunities not only enhances performance but also drives creativity and innovation within the team. As a result, teams that practice serendipity can gain a competitive edge by uncovering unique solutions and approaches that others may overlook. Ultimately, this openness to the unexpected can lead to breakthroughs that structured, planned efforts alone might not achieve.

Here is one example of when a team discovers an unexpected opportunity. A customer service team receives a call from a dissatisfied customer about a minor issue with a product. During the conversation, the customer mentions a unique way they use the product that the company had never considered. This insight sparks an idea among the team members to develop a new product feature or even a whole new product line that caters to this innovative use. By being open to unexpected feedback, the team discovers a new market opportunity that could lead to significant growth.

Foster a Culture of Curiosity

Additionally, practicing serendipity fosters a culture of curiosity and exploration within the team. When team members are encouraged to explore new ideas, even if they seem unrelated to their immediate goals, they are more likely to stumble upon creative solutions to problems. This culture of exploration helps to keep the team engaged and motivated, as it breaks the monotony of routine tasks and encourages a continuous search for improvement. It also promotes a learning environment where every experience, even those that appear to be failures, is seen as an opportunity to learn and grow. Here is one example of fostering a culture of curiosity through serendipity. At a company retreat, a group of employees from different departments strikes up a casual conversation about their hobbies and interests outside of work. One employee mentions a passion for virtual reality (VR), and another discusses their interest in user experience design. These unrelated interests lead to an impromptu brainstorming session about integrating VR into their current digital products to enhance user experience. This serendipitous conversation plants the seed for a groundbreaking project that combines VR with user experience design, ultimately leading to a successful new product launch.

Another example involves a software development team that is experimenting with a new programing language for a side project. Although the language is not directly related to their main product, they discover that it offers a more efficient way to handle a specific type of data processing. Realizing its potential, they decide to incorporate this new language into their primary development process, significantly improving the performance and scalability of their software. By being open to experimenting with new tools, the team uncovers an unexpected opportunity to innovate and enhance their product.

Enhance Collaboration

Lastly, serendipity can enhance collaboration within a team. When team members share their unexpected findings or insights, it encourages open communication and knowledge sharing. This collaborative spirit can strengthen relationships among team members and build trust, as everyone feels more involved in the collective journey toward success. By embracing the unpredictable nature of serendipity, high-performing teams can build resilience and agility, which are crucial qualities in navigating the uncertainties of today's business world.

Here is one example of enhancing collaboration within a team. A marketing team is monitoring social media for brand mentions when they notice a trending hashtag that aligns with their brand values. The team decides to spontaneously create and share content related to this trend, even though it was not part of their planned marketing strategy. The content quickly goes viral, attracting a new audience and generating increased engagement and sales. By being open to the serendipitous discovery of a relevant social media trend, the team is able to capitalize on an unexpected opportunity to drive growth.

Conclusion

Reflecting on the role of serendipity in the future, Priya Parker, author of *The Art of Gathering*, stated in an interview published in *The Wall Street Journal*: "In the future, serendipity will either be designed or dead. The great American cities were designed for run-ins, for bump-ins. In the office, we have open floor plans, hallways, and water coolers. The digital office planners of the 21st century will equally be designing for some of that spontaneity and serendipity."[2] One final observation about serendipity comes from Frans Johansson writing in the *Harvard Business Review*. While predicting trends, analyzing data, and gaming out strategies are often defined as the hallmarks of success, Johansson suggested, "if it was that simple we should have solved the mystery of success long time ago—and we haven't. Instead, serendipity is what sets us apart—since that is the only way we can discover an approach that is not obvious or logical.[3]

Self-Reflection Questions

1. How do I currently create opportunities for serendipitous communication in my workplace or personal environment?

2. Can I recall a time when an unexpected encounter or conversation led to a breakthrough idea or solution? What factors contributed to that moment?

3. In what ways do I remain open to unexpected opportunities in my daily work? How might I improve this openness?

4. How does my current workspace or routine encourage or hinder spontaneous interactions with colleagues or team members?

5. How often do I engage in conversations or activities unrelated to my immediate goals? What have I discovered from these explorations?

6. When faced with a new idea or challenge, how do I balance structured planning with the flexibility to pivot if new opportunities arise?

7. How can I foster a culture of curiosity and exploration within my team or peer group? What specific actions might I take?

8. What are some recent examples where collaboration within my team led to unexpected positive outcomes? How did serendipity play a role?

9. How do I approach failures or setbacks? Do I view them as opportunities to learn and grow, or do I tend to focus on the negatives?

10. How might I redesign my physical or virtual workspace to better encourage serendipitous interactions and collaboration with others?

CHAPTER 16

Prioritize Respect and Thoughtfulness

Introduction

In high-performing teams, the values of thoughtfulness and respect serve as foundational pillars that support trust, employee retention, and psychological safety. These teams understand that cultivating an environment where members feel secure and valued leads to stronger interpersonal connections, greater innovation, and sustained commitment to the organization. Trust, built on the consistent demonstration of thoughtfulness and respect, fosters open communication and collaboration, enabling teams to achieve their goals more effectively. Additionally, when team members feel respected, they are more likely to remain loyal to the organization, resulting in higher employee retention and a more stable, cohesive team. Furthermore, psychological safety, which thrives in a culture of respect, empowers individuals to share ideas and take risks without fear, driving both personal and collective growth. By prioritizing these values, high-performing teams not only enhance their own effectiveness but also contribute to the long-term success and resilience of the organization. Commenting on the essential skill of respect in high-performing teams, Marian Evans wrote in *Forbes*, "one of the most important elements of high-performing teams is the relationships between the people in them. Whether it's the relationships between colleagues or the employees and their leader, there's no team without trust, and that trust is built on a culture of psychological safety."[1]

Build Trust

Thoughtfulness and respect play a critical role in building trust within a team. When team members consistently demonstrate these values, they create an environment where individuals feel secure in their interactions. This security allows for open communication, where team members can share ideas, concerns, and feedback without fear of judgment. Trust developed through thoughtfulness and respect also encourages collaboration, as individuals are more likely to rely on and support one another. In turn, this mutual reliance strengthens the team's unity, creating a solid foundation for collective success. Furthermore, trust built on respect helps in resolving conflicts more effectively, as team members feel confident that their perspectives will be heard and valued. As trust deepens, it fosters a culture where team members are more likely to take risks, knowing that their team has their back. Ultimately, trust serves as the glue that holds high-performing teams together, enabling them to achieve their goals more efficiently.

When trust flourishes in a team, it positively impacts the team's overall performance. Members are more inclined to engage in productive discussions, knowing that their contributions will be respected. This sense of security leads to greater innovation, as individuals feel empowered to propose new ideas and approaches without fear of rejection. Additionally, trust minimizes the barriers to effective teamwork, such as misunderstandings or miscommunications, by promoting clear and honest dialogue. As a result, the team can move forward with a shared vision, making decisions that align with their collective goals. Trust also enhances accountability within the team, as members are more likely to follow through on their commitments when they know their peers are depending on them. In this way, thoughtfulness and respect not only build trust but also reinforce the team's commitment to excellence. The cycle of trust, supported by these core values, becomes self-sustaining, driving the team to higher levels of achievement.

Enhance Employee Retention

Thoughtfulness and respect significantly contribute to higher employee retention rates in teams. When individuals feel valued and respected within their team, they are more likely to experience job satisfaction and a sense of belonging. This positive work environment reduces the likelihood of employees seeking opportunities elsewhere, thereby decreasing turnover rates. High employee retention also benefits the organization by maintaining team stability, which is essential for long-term success. The costs associated with hiring and training new employees can be substantial, so retaining skilled and experienced team members saves the organization both time and money. Additionally, teams with low turnover tend to perform better, as continuity allows for deeper collaboration and a stronger understanding of team dynamics. When employees feel respected, they are more likely to stay committed to the organization's goals, contributing to its overall success. By prioritizing thoughtfulness and respect, organizations can create a culture that attracts and retains top talent.

Moreover, teams that emphasize thoughtfulness and respect often enjoy a more positive workplace culture, which further enhances employee retention. In such environments, employees are more engaged and motivated, as they feel that their contributions are genuinely appreciated. This sense of appreciation fosters loyalty, encouraging team members to invest more in their work and in the organization. Furthermore, a respectful atmosphere promotes open communication, allowing employees to voice their concerns or suggestions without fear of negative repercussions. This openness leads to better problem-solving and a more adaptive team, as issues are addressed proactively rather than being allowed to fester. High-performing teams that retain their members also benefit from the accumulated knowledge and experience that long-term employees bring, which can be a significant competitive advantage. In this way, the focus on thoughtfulness and respect not only boosts employee retention but also enhances the team's overall effectiveness and ability to innovate.

Promote Psychological Safety

Psychological safety is a key factor in creating a high-performing team, and it is deeply rooted in thoughtfulness and respect. When team members feel psychologically safe, they are more likely to share their ideas, even if those ideas are unconventional or carry some risk. This openness leads to a culture of innovation, where creativity is encouraged, and new solutions are explored. Thoughtfulness and respect contribute to this safety by ensuring that every team member's input is valued, regardless of their position or experience level. In such an environment, individuals are less likely to fear judgment or criticism, which reduces the barriers to effective communication. This sense of safety also encourages continuous learning, as team members feel comfortable admitting mistakes and seeking help when needed. As a result, the team becomes more resilient and adaptable, capable of navigating challenges with greater ease. Psychological safety, underpinned by thoughtfulness and respect, thus becomes a catalyst for both individual and collective growth within the team.

In addition to fostering innovation, psychological safety has a profound impact on team morale and well-being. When employees feel safe, they experience less stress and anxiety, leading to a more positive and productive work environment. Thoughtfulness and respect play a crucial role in reducing the fear of failure, which is often a significant source of workplace stress. By promoting a culture where mistakes are seen as opportunities for learning rather than reasons for punishment, teams can maintain high levels of morale and engagement. This positive atmosphere also strengthens relationships within the team, as members are more likely to support each other when they feel safe and respected. Furthermore, psychological safety encourages a sense of ownership and responsibility, as team members feel more invested in their work and the outcomes of their efforts. Over time, this leads to a more cohesive and high-performing team, where each individual feels empowered to contribute to the team's success.

Self-Reflection Questions

1. How do I demonstrate thoughtfulness and respect in my interactions with team members, and how might this impact the level of trust within the team?

2. In what ways can I contribute to creating a work environment where everyone feels secure and valued, thereby fostering stronger interpersonal connections?

3. How do I respond to feedback and concerns from colleagues? Do my actions encourage open communication and collaboration?

4. What steps can I take to help build a culture of psychological safety in my team, where individuals feel comfortable sharing ideas and taking risks?

5. How do I contribute to or hinder the retention of skilled team members by either promoting or neglecting thoughtfulness and respect?

6. Do I actively work to ensure that my team members feel appreciated and respected, and how does this impact their motivation and commitment to the team's goals?

7. How do I handle conflicts within the team? Do I approach them in a way that builds trust and reinforces a respectful environment?

8. In what ways have I seen thoughtfulness and respect positively influence the team's performance, and how can I further encourage these values?

9. How do I help create an environment where mistakes are seen as learning opportunities, thus reducing fear and promoting psychological safety?

10. What personal actions or behaviors could I improve to better contribute to a team culture that prioritizes trust, retention, and psychological safety?

CHAPTER 17

Practice Self-Care and Self-Love

Introduction

The practice of self-care and self-love has become an essential skill for high-performing teams, particularly in leveraging strategies such as promoting work–life balance and boundaries, encouraging healthy habits and practices, and providing resources and support for managing stress and prioritizing self-care. Each of these strategies contributes to the overall well-being and efficiency of the team, fostering a healthier work environment and enhancing productivity. As one author noted, "investing in employee well-being not only enhances individual productivity and satisfaction but also delivers substantial returns for the organization."[1]

Promoting Work–Life Balance and Boundaries

Promoting work–life balance and boundaries within a team is crucial for maintaining high performance. Teams that recognize the importance of setting clear boundaries between work and personal life can reduce burnout and increase job satisfaction. The results of the American Psychological Association's *2023 Work in America Survey* confirmed that psychological well-being is a very high priority for workers themselves. The survey found that 92 percent of workers said that it is very (57%) or somewhat (35%) important to them to work for an organization that values their emotional and psychological well-being.[2] Moreover, 92 percent of employees said that it is very (52%) or somewhat (40%) important to them to work for an organization that provides support for employee mental health.[3] In short, employees who experience a healthy work–life balance tend to have better well-being, lower stress levels, and higher job satisfaction. Encouraging team members to set limits on their work hours and take regular breaks can help prevent burnout and maintain motivation. Leadership plays a key role in fostering this environment by modeling balanced behaviors and emphasizing the importance of personal time.

Organizations can enhance employee well-being by implementing policies that promote work–life balance, such as flexible working hours, remote work options, and mandatory time off. These policies help employees manage their personal and professional responsibilities more effectively, which can lead to a more motivated and engaged workforce. Additionally, technology can support work–life balance by improving time management and communication without overwhelming employees. Tools such as project management software keep teams organized and on track, while communication platforms that allow for asynchronous interactions reduce the need for constant availability. By adopting these strategies, organizations can create a healthier work environment that supports both productivity and overall well-being.

Encouraging Healthy Habits and Practices

Encouraging healthy habits and practices that support well-being is a vital strategy for any team. Teams that prioritize physical health, such as through regular exercise and a balanced diet, as well as mental health practices such as mindfulness and meditation, are better equipped to handle workplace challenges. A 2023 article in *Harvard Business Review* emphasized that integrating wellness programs that promote both physical and mental health can lead to improved employee performance and reduced absenteeism.[4] By fostering an environment where healthy habits are encouraged, teams can build resilience and sustain high levels of performance over the long term.[5] Wellness programs might include fitness challenges, healthy eating initiatives, and mental health support to create a culture that values overall well-being. This approach helps teams not only enhance their physical health but also boost mental clarity and emotional stability. Encouraging these practices can significantly improve both individual and team performance.

Moreover, mental health practices are equally crucial in maintaining a balanced and productive workplace. Encouraging mindfulness and meditation can help team members manage stress and improve focus. Providing resources such as guided meditation sessions, mindfulness workshops, and access to mental health apps supports these practices and promotes a healthy work environment. Additionally, fostering a supportive environment where healthy habits are celebrated can reinforce these behaviors. Recognizing and rewarding employees who make healthy lifestyle choices, such as participating in wellness challenges or consistently practicing mindfulness, can motivate others to follow suit. This not only enhances individual well-being but also cultivates a culture of health and wellness within the team. By integrating these strategies, organizations can ensure that their teams are well-equipped to meet both personal and professional challenges.

Providing Resources and Support for Managing Stress

Providing resources and support for managing stress and prioritizing self-care is crucial for high-performing teams. Access to counseling services, stress management workshops, and self-care tools can greatly enhance an employee's ability to cope with workplace pressures. By ensuring that team members have the necessary support to manage stress, organizations can foster a more positive and productive work environment. Companies prioritizing mental health resources see significant improvements in employee well-being and performance. Managing stress effectively helps prevent burnout and reduces absenteeism, contributing to sustained high performance. Comprehensive wellness programs that include stress management and self-care tools equip employees with the skills they need to maintain their well-being. Such initiatives are essential for fostering a resilient and motivated workforce. As Stephen Sokoler wrote in a July 30, 2024 *Forbes* article, "investing in employee mental health is not only a moral imperative but a strategic business move. Companies that prioritize mental well-being can expect to see improvements in productivity, employee engagement, retention and overall corporate reputation."[6]

In addition to formal resources, creating a supportive work environment where employees feel comfortable discussing their stressors is vital. This can be achieved by fostering open communication and providing a safe space for employees to share their concerns. Encouraging a culture where employees feel valued and supported can lead to improved morale and productivity. Promoting informal support networks within the team can also strengthen these efforts. By encouraging team members to support each other and share stress management strategies, organizations can build a sense of camaraderie and collective resilience. This not only helps individuals manage stress more effectively but also enhances overall team cohesion and performance. By integrating both formal and informal support systems, companies can create a healthier and more dynamic workplace.

Conclusion

Fostering self-care and self-love in high-performing teams is essential for creating a productive and healthy work environment. Strategies such as promoting work–life balance, encouraging healthy habits, and providing resources for stress management are vital to maintaining team well-being. These approaches help prevent burnout, enhance job satisfaction, and improve overall team morale. Implementing flexible work policies, supporting mental health practices, and offering stress management resources equip employees with tools to thrive. By integrating these practices, organizations can build a resilient workforce that is motivated, engaged, and capable of handling both personal and professional challenges.

Self-Reflection Questions

1. How do I currently balance my work and personal life to prevent burnout?

2. What boundaries have I set to ensure a healthy work–life balance?
3. In what ways do I practice self-care to maintain my well-being?
4. How often do I take breaks during my workday to recharge and avoid stress?
5. What healthy habits have I incorporated into my daily routine?
6. How do I manage stress effectively in my professional life?
7. Do I encourage my team members to practice self-care and set healthy boundaries?
8. How do I support my colleagues in maintaining their mental and emotional well-being?
9. What resources or support systems do I use to manage work-related stress?
10. How can I improve my approach to self-care and self-love to enhance my performance and well-being?

CHAPTER 18

Nurture Equanimity in Your Life and Work

Introduction

Nurturing equanimity in life and work is an essential skill for high-performing teams, particularly when leveraging strategies such as fostering a sense of calm and balance in the face of challenges and uncertainty, encouraging mindfulness practices and techniques for managing emotions, and building team empathy. These strategies contribute significantly to the stability and effectiveness of a team, ensuring that they remain focused, cohesive, and productive even in the most challenging circumstances. As Toni Bernhard noted: "Equanimity is an even-tempered state of mind that enables you to ride life's challenges with calmness and serenity, instead of being tossed about like a ship in a storm."[1] Since most organizations face a constant sense of stress in today's VUCA global marketplace, many employees feel like they are being tossed about like a ship in a storm. For high-performing teams, then, nurturing equanimity in their life and work is the next essential skill.

Foster a Sense of Calm and Balance in the Face of Challenges and Uncertainty

Fostering a sense of calm and balance in the face of challenges is essential for maintaining team performance. Teams that can stay composed under pressure are better equipped to think clearly, make informed decisions, and mitigate the negative effects of stress. A sense of calm can be cultivated through practices such as deep breathing exercises, regular breaks, and creating an environment where team members feel safe expressing concerns. Leadership also plays a crucial role in this process. Leaders who demonstrate calmness and balanced decision making set a strong example for their teams, encouraging them to adopt similar approaches.

Structured team-building activities that focus on relaxation and stress relief, such as group meditation sessions, nature retreats, and yoga classes, are effective methods for fostering calm. These activities not only provide immediate stress relief but also teach techniques that team members can use individually to maintain calm in stressful situations. Incorporating such practices into the workplace can significantly enhance team cohesion and resilience under pressure. By prioritizing these strategies, organizations can create a supportive environment that promotes well-being and sustained high performance. For example, McKinsey reported that during times of crises leaders should "act with deliberate calm and bounded optimism. Those who can visibly demonstrate these qualities help their organizations feel a sense of purpose, giving them hope that they can face the challenges ahead."[2]

Encourage Mindfulness Practices and Techniques for Managing Emotions

Encouraging mindfulness practices and techniques for managing emotions is a vital strategy for cultivating equanimity in high-performing teams. Mindfulness involves being fully present and engaged in the moment, helping team members manage their emotions and reduce stress. By incorporating mindfulness techniques such as meditation, mindful breathing, and body scans into the daily routine, teams can enhance their ability to remain focused and calm under pressure. Additionally, training programs and workshops on emotional intelligence and mindfulness can equip team members with skills to manage their emotions effectively, fostering a supportive and empathetic environment.

Integrating mindfulness practices into daily work routines can further reinforce these benefits. Simple practices such as starting meetings with a brief mindfulness exercise or having quiet spaces for meditation can make mindfulness a regular part of the workday.

Researchers writing in the *Harvard Business Review* discussed how mindfulness practices can significantly reduce conflict and enhance team performance by fostering a collective awareness of present experiences. "When team members focus on mindfulness, they are less likely to engage in harmful relationship conflicts and more likely to maintain productive task conflicts."[3] Additionally, high-performing teams that practice mindfulness "are better at managing stress and maintaining focus, which can lead to improved outcomes and reduced emotional friction. Implementing mindfulness strategies can help teams navigate challenges more effectively and support a more cohesive work environment."[4]

Building Team Empathy

Over the last decade, as the world has grown more complicated and markets around the globe have had to adjust to one technological advancement after another, "organizations have invested a great deal of time, money, and effort in teaching executives to be more empathetic. Studies show a strong positive correlation between direct reports' accounts of their manager's empathy and the ratings the manager receives from their own boss."[5] In short, "empathic leaders make for better leaders."[6] High-performing teams have leaders who understand the need to build team empathy by having everyone support one another during difficult times because mutual support enhances resilience, builds trust, and fosters a collaborative environment. When employees support each other, they can better manage stress and challenges, leading to improved overall performance. This support can take various forms, such as offering emotional encouragement, sharing workloads, or providing constructive feedback. By creating an environment where team members feel safe and valued, teams can maintain high morale and productivity even during tough periods. Encouraging open communication and empathy among team members strengthens relationships and ensures that everyone feels connected and supported.

Building such team empathy is even more important now that the age of AI is upon us and moving faster with each passing day. For those who believe that AI will monopolize the future of work, thus leaving humans out of a functional role, they may ask, "in this period of AI, does empathy at work still matter?" Yes, even more so. "As technology does more and more, we're barreling toward a world where behaviors like empathy become the *only* thing that matters."[7] The Capgemini Research Institute published research and concluded that "as the use of AI began to hit an inflection point found that an organization's need for the entire spectrum of emotional intelligence might become up to six times greater as routine tasks are automated, leaving only the more emotionally challenging jobs for human workers."[8] Today, as the AI journey truly takes off, building an empathic organization can begin to unlock the full spectrum of emotionally intelligent behaviors.

Conclusion

Nurturing equanimity in high-performing teams is essential for maintaining stability and effectiveness, particularly when facing challenges and uncertainty. Strategies such as fostering calm, encouraging mindfulness, and building empathy help teams stay focused, cohesive, and productive. Leaders who model equanimity and promote a supportive environment can enhance resilience and adaptability among team members. Additionally, mindfulness practices and emotional intelligence training can reduce stress and improve emotional regulation. Building team empathy fosters mutual support and trust, which are crucial in managing stress and overcoming challenges. As teams navigate the evolving workplace landscape, these skills become even more valuable for sustained high performance.

Self-Reflection Questions

1. How do I foster a sense of calm and balance in my daily work routine?
2. What specific strategies do I use to manage stress and maintain composure under pressure?
3. How do I encourage mindfulness practices among my team members?

4. In what ways do I model equanimity and emotional regulation for my team?

5. How can I improve my approach to building empathy within the team?

6. What steps do I take to create a supportive and trusting team environment?

7. How effectively do I facilitate open communication and understanding in my team?

8. How do I help my team members feel safe expressing their concerns and emotions?

9. What team-building activities have been successful in promoting relaxation and stress relief?

10. How can I further develop emotional intelligence skills within myself and my team to navigate challenges effectively?

CHAPTER 19

Focus on the Present Moment

Introduction

In today's fast-paced and demanding work environments, high-performing teams must develop and refine essential skills that enable them to maintain peak productivity and effectiveness. One such critical skill is the ability to focus on the present moment. Focusing on the present moment involves more than just paying attention; it requires cultivating awareness of current market conditions, fostering a culture of concentration, and promoting continuous awareness of the here and now. These strategies help teams manage their workload, enhance collaboration, and improve overall performance. The following sections delve into how high-performing teams can successfully implement these strategies to thrive in a competitive landscape.

Cultivating Awareness of Current Market Conditions

High-performing teams cultivate awareness of current market conditions to stay competitive and make informed decisions that align with their strategic objectives. By continuously monitoring market trends, customer preferences, and competitor actions, teams can anticipate shifts that may impact their organization. This proactive approach allows them to adjust their strategies promptly, ensuring that they remain relevant and effective in their respective industries. For example, staying updated on emerging technologies or regulatory changes can help teams innovate or pivot their offerings to better meet market demands. Moreover, awareness of market conditions fosters agility, enabling teams to respond swiftly to opportunities or threats. This adaptability is crucial in today's fast-paced environment, where market dynamics can change rapidly and unpredictably.

Furthermore, cultivating awareness of market conditions enhances collaboration and alignment within the team. When all members are informed about external factors influencing the business, they can contribute more effectively to strategy discussions and decision-making processes. This shared understanding minimizes silos and ensures that every team member is working toward a common goal, aligned with market realities. Additionally, it empowers teams to prioritize tasks and allocate resources more efficiently, focusing on high-impact initiatives that drive competitive advantage. In this way, being aware of the current market landscape not only enhances team performance but also strengthens the organization's position in the marketplace. Teams that consistently monitor and analyze market conditions can sustain long-term growth by staying ahead of trends and customer needs.

Fostering a Culture of Focus and Attention to the Task at Hand

Creating a culture where focus and attention are prioritized is essential for high-performing teams. This involves establishing clear goals, minimizing distractions, and promoting a work environment that values deep work. As Cal Newport discusses in his book *Deep Work: Rules for Focused Success in a Distracted World* (2021), "deep work is the ability to focus without distraction on a cognitively demanding task, which is a crucial skill in an economy that rewards complex and creative problem-solving."[1] Teams that cultivate this ability can tackle complex projects more efficiently, yielding higher quality results. By prioritizing deep work, teams can maximize their cognitive capabilities, enabling them to innovate and solve problems effectively. This culture not only enhances productivity but also contributes to job satisfaction and engagement, as employees find more meaning and fulfillment in their work.

Leaders play a pivotal role in fostering a culture of focus by setting expectations and modeling focused behavior. They can establish norms that encourage deep work, such as scheduling uninterrupted work periods and minimizing unnecessary meetings. Additionally, creating quiet workspaces and implementing policies that reduce distractions can help teams maintain concentration. These practices ensure that team members have the environment and support they need to engage in deep work. By emphasizing the importance of focus and attention, leaders can help their teams develop habits that lead to sustained high performance. In turn, this creates a more cohesive and productive work environment where everyone is aligned with the organization's goals and values. A focused team is better equipped to respond to challenges and seize opportunities, driving overall success.

To fully realize the benefits of a focus-centered culture, it is also important to consider the role of technology. Tools that help manage digital distractions and track time spent on various tasks can support employees in maintaining their focus. By using apps that block nonessential notifications, teams can reduce the cognitive load associated with task-switching and improve efficiency. Furthermore, investing in training that emphasizes the value of deep work can reinforce these practices. As Newport highlights, organizations that prioritize deep work can significantly outperform their competitors by leveraging the full cognitive capabilities of their workforce. Therefore, fostering a culture that values focus and attention involves a comprehensive approach, integrating leadership, environment, and technology to create a more effective and satisfying workplace.

Promoting Awareness of the Here and Now to Maximize Productivity and Effectiveness

Promoting awareness of the present moment, often known as present-moment awareness, is a powerful strategy that can significantly enhance a team's productivity and effectiveness. This practice involves being fully engaged with the current task, free from the distractions of past concerns or future anxieties. By focusing on what is happening right now, team members can better manage their attention and energy, leading to more effective and efficient work. This approach helps individuals to fully immerse themselves in their tasks, reducing the risk of errors and improving the quality of their output. Moreover, present-moment awareness encourages a mindful approach to work, which can help individuals handle immediate challenges more effectively. This mindful engagement can also foster a sense of satisfaction and fulfillment, as team members feel more connected to their work. As a result, cultivating present-moment awareness within a team can lead to higher job performance and overall job satisfaction.

Incorporating present-moment awareness into a team's daily routine can lead to numerous benefits beyond individual performance. Teams can cultivate this awareness by implementing regular check-ins and reflections, allowing members to pause and assess their current state. This practice helps them realign their focus and energy, ensuring that they remain grounded and attentive to their tasks. Techniques such as time-blocking and task batching can further support this approach by minimizing distractions and reducing the cognitive load associated with multitasking. By scheduling specific periods for focused work and grouping similar tasks together, teams can maintain a high level of concentration and productivity. Additionally, promoting a culture that values mindfulness and present-moment awareness can enhance teamwork and collaboration. When team members are mindful, they communicate more effectively, develop stronger interpersonal connections, and work more cohesively. Integrating mindfulness practices, such as meditation and breathing exercises, into the daily routine can further reinforce this culture, helping team members manage stress and maintain a balanced perspective.

One example of a company that helped employees focus to increase productivity was Unilever. In today's fast-paced work environment, distractions are everywhere, posing a serious threat to productivity and focus. To combat this, companies like Unilever have successfully implemented mindfulness programs that improved employees' attention spans by 30 percent.[2] Through guided meditation sessions and the practice of present-moment awareness, employees not only reduced errors but also experienced increased satisfaction and creativity. This initiative highlights the powerful impact that a culture of mindfulness can have in countering the constant barrage of modern distractions. The benefits extend beyond just productivity, fostering a more engaged and creative workforce. Thus, prioritizing mindfulness in the workplace can serve as an effective strategy to enhance overall employee well-being and performance.

Conclusion

Developing a high-performing team in today's fast-paced work environment requires a strong focus on present-moment awareness, awareness of market conditions, and a culture that prioritizes deep work. By fostering these skills, teams can enhance their productivity and effectiveness, enabling them to handle complex tasks more efficiently and make informed decisions that align with strategic objectives. This approach not only helps in managing workload but also promotes collaboration and innovation by encouraging team members to stay engaged and attentive. A culture of deep work, supported by leadership and appropriate tools, ensures that teams remain focused on their tasks, reducing errors and improving the quality of output. Moreover, integrating mindfulness practices into daily routines helps maintain a balanced perspective, reduces stress, and enhances overall job satisfaction. As organizations continue to navigate a rapidly changing market, the ability to focus on the present and adapt quickly will remain crucial. Ultimately, by cultivating these practices, teams can build a more cohesive, resilient, and high-performing work environment that drives long-term success.

Self-Reflection Questions

1. How often do I focus on the present moment when working, and how does this impact my productivity?
2. What strategies do I use to stay aware of current market conditions in my industry, and how do they inform my decision making?
3. In what ways do I contribute to fostering a culture of concentration within my team or organization?
4. How do I balance staying informed about market trends with maintaining focus on immediate tasks?

5. What practices can I implement to minimize distractions and enhance my ability to engage in deep work?

6. How do I currently manage my workload, and what improvements could help me handle tasks more effectively?

7. How can I encourage my team to incorporate mindfulness practices into our daily routines to enhance focus and collaboration?

8. In what ways can I adjust my approach to work to better align with my organization's strategic objectives?

9. How do I support my team in cultivating a shared understanding of external factors that influence our business?

10. What steps can I take to integrate mindfulness and present-moment awareness into both my professional and personal life?

CHAPTER 20

Create an Authentic Sense of Self

Introduction

High-performing teams thrive when they cultivate an authentic sense of self among employees, which is essential for enhancing engagement, reducing turnover, and improving well-being. Encouraging employees to express their true selves at work fosters deeper engagement, as they feel more connected to their roles and motivated to contribute to the team's success. This increased engagement drives productivity and creativity, leading to better overall performance. Additionally, when employees feel authentic and valued, they are less likely to leave the organization, resulting in reduced turnover and higher retention rates. This stability allows teams to maintain continuity and build strong, trusting relationships that enhance collaboration. Moreover, promoting authenticity supports employee well-being by reducing stress and anxiety, creating a healthier and more balanced work environment. A team that prioritizes authenticity not only improves individual satisfaction but also strengthens the overall team dynamic, leading to sustained success. This essential skill of creating an authentic sense of self is a strategic imperative for organizations around the globe as "62 percent of workers report being not engaged (unattached to their jobs and company) and 15 percent are actively disengaged (undermining the progress of their company out of resentment). European workers report the least engagement, with only 13 percent expressing interest in their work."[1]

Enhanced Employee Engagement

Enhanced employee engagement is crucial for high-performing teams because it drives both individual and collective success. When employees feel empowered to express their authentic selves, they are more likely to experience a deep connection to their work. This authenticity fosters a sense of belonging and purpose, which motivates employees to invest more in their tasks and the team's overall success. Engaged employees are typically more enthusiastic about their work, leading to higher levels of creativity and innovation. They are more inclined to take initiative, seek out opportunities for improvement, and contribute meaningfully to team objectives. This proactive attitude not only boosts individual performance but also enhances team dynamics, as members feel more connected and aligned with one another. Moreover, engagement can lead to a more positive workplace culture, where employees are supportive of each other and collaborate more effectively. When all team members are fully engaged, the team is better positioned to achieve its goals and deliver exceptional results.

Additionally, employee engagement enhances productivity and efficiency within high-performing teams. Engaged employees are more likely to stay focused on their tasks, minimize distractions, and maintain a high level of concentration. This focus enables them to complete their work more efficiently, reducing the time spent on each task and increasing overall output. Furthermore, engaged employees often display a stronger commitment to quality, striving to deliver the best possible results in every project they undertake. Their dedication to their roles and responsibilities contributes to a more robust and reliable team performance. Engagement also fosters resilience, as employees who are deeply involved in their work are better equipped to handle challenges and setbacks. They are more likely to view obstacles as opportunities for growth rather than insurmountable barriers. In turn, this resilience strengthens the team's ability to navigate complex situations and maintain high performance, even under pressure. Ultimately, enhanced employee engagement through authenticity is a key factor in building a cohesive, motivated, and high-performing team.

Reduced Turnover and Increased Retention

Reduced turnover and increased retention are critical benefits of fostering an authentic sense of self in high-performing teams. When employees feel that they can be their authentic selves at work, they are more likely to develop a deeper connection to the organization and its values. This sense of belonging and acceptance makes employees feel valued and respected, which significantly reduces the likelihood of burnout and turnover. High retention rates are particularly important for high-performing teams, as they allow for continuity and stability in operations. Retaining experienced employees ensures that the team maintains its collective knowledge, skills, and competencies, which are crucial for sustaining high performance over time. Furthermore, high retention minimizes the disruption caused by frequent employee turnover, allowing teams to focus on their goals without the constant need to integrate new members. This stability is essential for building trust and cohesion among team members, which further enhances overall team performance. Additionally, long-term employees are more likely to align with the team's culture and values, fostering a more harmonious and collaborative work environment.

Increased retention also has significant cost-saving implications for organizations. When turnover is low, companies save on the expenses associated with recruiting, hiring, and training new employees. These savings can be substantial, especially when considering the time and resources needed to onboard new hires and bring them up to speed. Moreover, by retaining skilled and experienced employees, organizations can avoid the productivity dips that often accompany new hires learning the ropes. This continuity helps maintain momentum on projects and ensures that teams remain focused on achieving their objectives. In addition, employees who feel secure in their roles are more likely to invest in their personal and professional development, further enhancing their value to the organization. By reducing turnover and increasing retention through authenticity, high-performing teams can build a solid foundation of experienced, motivated, and engaged employees who contribute to long-term success. Overall, fostering an environment where employees feel comfortable being their authentic selves is a powerful strategy for maintaining a stable, high-performing team.

Enhanced Employee Well-Being

Enhanced employee well-being is a critical aspect of creating an authentic sense of self, which significantly contributes to the effectiveness of high-performing teams. When employees are allowed to be authentic at work, they experience a profound sense of relief from not having to conform to a false persona. This authenticity reduces stress and anxiety, leading to better mental and emotional well-being. A healthy work environment where employees feel free to express their true selves fosters a positive atmosphere, enhancing overall morale. When individuals are less burdened by the need to present a particular image, they are more likely to be satisfied and content in their roles. This sense of well-being enables employees to focus better on their tasks and responsibilities, resulting in increased productivity and efficiency. Furthermore, a workplace that promotes authenticity encourages open communication and strong interpersonal relationships, which are key to building trust and collaboration among team members. When employees feel mentally and emotionally healthy, they are more resilient and better equipped to handle workplace challenges. As a result, teams with high employee well-being are more adaptable and can maintain high performance even under pressure.

Additionally, promoting a culture of authenticity and well-being can lead to long-term benefits for both employees and organizations. When employees feel valued and supported in their authentic selves, they are more likely to develop a strong sense of loyalty to the organization. This loyalty translates to lower turnover rates and higher retention, preserving the collective experience and knowledge within the team. Moreover, a focus on employee well-being can reduce absenteeism and presenteeism, ensuring that the team operates at full capacity. Employees who feel psychologically safe and supported are more likely to take risks and innovate, contributing to the team's overall success. A positive work environment that prioritizes well-being also attracts top talent, as individuals are drawn to organizations where they can thrive both personally and professionally. By fostering a culture that values authenticity and well-being, high-performing teams can sustain a motivated and engaged workforce. This approach not only enhances team dynamics but also drives long-term success and growth for the organization. Ultimately, investing in employee well-being is a strategic move that benefits everyone involved, leading to a healthier, more productive, and successful workplace.

Conclusion

Cultivating an authentic sense of self among employees is essential for building high-performing teams that thrive in today's competitive landscape. With 58 percent of global workers reporting that they are struggling, and with employee well-being declining especially among young people, this essential skill of high-performing teams of encouraging an authentic sense of self remains critical moving forward.[2] By promoting authenticity, organizations can enhance employee engagement, leading to greater productivity, creativity, and a stronger connection to the team's goals. This approach also significantly reduces turnover and increases retention, allowing teams to maintain stability and continuity while preserving valuable knowledge and skills. Additionally, fostering authenticity supports employee well-being by reducing stress and promoting a healthier work–life balance, which is crucial for sustaining high performance. When employees feel valued and respected for who they are, they are more likely to be motivated, committed, and resilient, contributing to a positive and collaborative work environment. This creates a solid foundation for long-term success, as teams are better equipped to innovate, adapt, and achieve their objectives. Ultimately, prioritizing an authentic sense of self is a strategic imperative that benefits both employees and the organization, driving overall effectiveness and growth.

Self-Reflection Questions

1. How comfortable do I feel expressing my true self at work, and how does this impact my engagement with my tasks and team?

2. In what ways does feeling valued and respected by my team and organization influence my decision to stay or leave?

3. How often do I find myself pretending to be someone I'm not at work, and what effect does this have on my stress levels and overall well-being?

4. What specific actions can I take to foster a more authentic and open environment for myself and my colleagues?

5. How does being part of a team that values authenticity enhance my creativity and willingness to take initiative?

6. Do I feel that my workplace encourages open communication and strong interpersonal relationships? Why or why not?

7. How does my sense of authenticity at work affect my ability to handle challenges and setbacks?

8. In what ways do I contribute to building a positive and supportive workplace culture that values authenticity?

9. How does the sense of stability and continuity in my team influence my job satisfaction and performance?

10. What changes could be made in my work environment to better support my mental and emotional well-being through authenticity?

CHAPTER 21

Grow by Taking Calculated Risks

Introduction

High-performing teams thrive when they practice the essential skill of taking calculated risks. This ability not only drives innovation and problem-solving but also fosters deeper team dynamics that promote confidence, ownership, competitive advantage, and leadership growth. By analyzing the potential outcomes and making informed decisions, these teams transform risks into opportunities for development and success. Building confidence and ownership, enhancing competitive advantage, and developing leadership skills are three benefits for high-performing teams that take calculated risks.

Builds Confidence and Ownership

When high-performing teams take calculated risks and achieve positive results, it profoundly boosts their confidence. Team members become more assured in their abilities to navigate uncertainty and make informed decisions. This newfound confidence creates a ripple effect across the team, fostering an environment where individuals feel empowered to contribute more actively to projects and initiatives. They understand that their input is valued and impactful, motivating them to invest greater energy and creativity in their work. Confidence built through successful risk-taking also encourages individuals to take more ownership of their responsibilities. When people see their efforts contributing to the team's success, they develop a stronger sense of accountability for their roles. Moreover, team members are more likely to step up, propose new ideas, and solve problems independently when they trust in their own abilities. In turn, this culture of confidence strengthens the overall performance and cohesion of the team.

In addition to fostering confidence, calculated risks also help team members develop a deeper sense of ownership. As individuals become more responsible for outcomes, they gain a greater understanding of how their work aligns with the team's goals and the organization's broader vision. This sense of ownership increases engagement and commitment to delivering high-quality work because people feel that their efforts make a tangible difference. When team members feel accountable, they also become more invested in learning from both successes and failures. This willingness to reflect on outcomes builds resilience and encourages personal growth. By taking ownership, individuals are more likely to collaborate proactively, offer solutions, and mentor others, further enriching the team's capabilities. Ownership also drives continuous improvement, as team members are more inclined to refine their processes and approaches, leading to sustained team performance over time. As Anna Barnhill noted in *Forbes*: "Cultivating courage requires leaders to embrace vulnerability, take calculated risks, and champion bold ideas. Encouraging risk-taking and healthy debate within a safe framework is crucial for innovation and dynamic problem-solving."[1]

Enhances Competitive Advantage

Teams that regularly practice taking calculated risks are better positioned to gain a competitive advantage in the marketplace. This is because they develop a sharper ability to identify emerging trends and opportunities before their competitors do. By analyzing data, market conditions, and customer needs, these teams can take proactive steps to implement new strategies, products, or services that address unmet demands. This forward-thinking approach allows them to stay ahead of the curve and capture market share more effectively. In an ever-changing business landscape, organizations that are risk-averse may miss out on key opportunities, while teams that embrace calculated risks are more agile and responsive. This agility enables them to pivot quickly when new opportunities arise or when market conditions shift, giving them an edge over slower-moving competitors.

Moreover, calculated risk-taking enables high-performing teams to differentiate themselves in saturated markets. When a team is willing to experiment with new ideas and approaches, they are more likely to innovate and offer unique value propositions that set them apart. For example, they may introduce cutting-edge technology, streamline operational processes, or create personalized customer experiences, all of which can lead to increased customer loyalty and brand recognition. Furthermore, by consistently taking smart risks, teams build a reputation for being bold and forward-thinking, which can attract top talent and investors who are looking for organizations that are unafraid to push boundaries. Ultimately, a culture of calculated risk-taking becomes a powerful competitive tool that accelerates success, allowing the team and organization to maintain a leadership position in their industry.

Develops Leadership Skills

Taking calculated risks plays a pivotal role in developing leadership skills within high-performing teams. When individuals are given the opportunity to lead initiatives that involve risk, they learn how to assess situations holistically, make strategic decisions, and manage uncertainty. This process requires critical thinking and the ability to weigh potential benefits against drawbacks, sharpening the decision-making skills that are essential for effective leadership. Moreover, risk-taking allows emerging leaders to practice resilience by learning from both the successes and failures of their decisions. Each experience teaches valuable lessons in accountability, strategic planning, and team management, all of which contribute to personal and professional growth. As individuals gain more experience leading risk-related initiatives, they build the confidence needed to take on larger leadership roles within the organization.

Additionally, calculated risk-taking fosters a culture of leadership development across the entire team. When team members see their peers stepping up to lead initiatives, they are inspired to do the same, creating a ripple effect of leadership growth. Teams that regularly embrace risk encourage individuals to take ownership of projects, mentor others, and make strategic decisions that influence the direction of the organization. This environment empowers everyone, not just designated leaders, to think and act like leaders. As a result, the team develops a deep pool of leadership talent that can be relied upon in times of transition or when scaling the organization. Furthermore, these leadership experiences prepare individuals to guide the team through complex and high-stakes scenarios, ensuring that the team remains adaptable, resilient, and capable of handling future challenges.

Conclusion

High-performing teams benefit significantly from practicing the essential skill of taking calculated risks, as it drives innovation, strengthens team dynamics, and fosters leadership growth. By weighing potential outcomes and making informed decisions, teams can transform risks into opportunities for success. One key benefit is that taking calculated risks builds confidence and ownership among team members. When risks lead to positive outcomes, individuals feel empowered and motivated to take more responsibility, increasing their engagement and performance. Another benefit is that risk-taking enhances a team's competitive advantage. Teams that embrace risk are better positioned to identify opportunities before competitors, allowing them to stay agile and responsive in a fast-paced market. Additionally, calculated risk-taking develops leadership skills by allowing team members to step up, manage uncertainty, and practice decision making, ultimately cultivating a deep pool of leadership talent. Together, these benefits help teams remain innovative, resilient, and successful in navigating challenges and achieving long-term goals.

Self-Reflection Questions

1. How has taking calculated risks in my team projects boosted my confidence in making decisions and navigating uncertainty?

2. In what ways have I seen my sense of ownership increase after contributing to a successful risk-based initiative, and how has it impacted my performance?

3. How do I ensure that my input is valued and impactful when participating in team projects that involve calculated risks?

4. How has my team's culture of confidence and accountability evolved as a result of taking calculated risks together?

5. What steps do I take to align my work with the broader goals of the team and organization when taking ownership of a project?

6. How do I and my team identify emerging trends and opportunities that provide us with a competitive edge in a fast-paced market?

7. In what ways have calculated risks helped my team stand out from competitors or differentiate ourselves in saturated markets?

8. How have I developed leadership skills, such as decision making and resilience, through taking calculated risks in team initiatives?

9. What strategies do I use to mentor others and encourage leadership development in my team, particularly in risk-related projects?

10. How do I manage uncertainty and sharpen my critical thinking skills when leading or participating in projects that involve calculated risks?

CHAPTER 22

Understand the Dynamics of Stress

Introduction

High-performing teams thrive when they understand and manage the dynamics of stress, an essential skill that profoundly impacts communication, team cohesion, and overall well-being. In fast-paced work environments, stress is inevitable, but how teams respond to it can determine their success. Mastering stress dynamics enables teams to not only handle challenges effectively but also enhance their collaboration, resilience, and long-term performance. Teams that proactively manage stress are not only better prepared to navigate crises but also build a culture of trust and open communication. This understanding translates into clear communication during high-pressure situations, stronger bonds among team members, and a focus on mental and physical health. By cultivating this skill, teams are better equipped to navigate both routine tasks and crises, leading to greater productivity and sustained success.

Enhanced Communication

Effective communication is crucial for high-performing teams, especially during stressful situations. When stress levels rise, team members may misinterpret messages, respond emotionally, or withdraw from discussions. However, teams that understand the dynamics of stress can recognize when these patterns arise and implement strategies to improve communication. By practicing active listening and maintaining emotional control, team members are more likely to express their thoughts clearly and respond thoughtfully. Understanding stress also helps teams manage conflict, as they can address misunderstandings before they escalate. In tense moments, members are less likely to react defensively or aggressively, fostering a more supportive and constructive dialogue. Additionally, stress management allows for more empathetic communication, as members are better able to understand the pressures their colleagues may be facing. Overall, mastering stress dynamics ensures that high-performing teams maintain effective communication, even in the most challenging circumstances.

When stress is properly managed, communication becomes more intentional and solution-focused. High-performing teams that practice stress management are less prone to reactive behaviors, such as interrupting or making assumptions about what others mean. Instead, they take the time to clarify and confirm messages, reducing the risk of miscommunication. Additionally, these teams are better at balancing assertiveness with empathy, ensuring that all voices are heard without letting emotions dominate the conversation. Clear communication during stressful times also leads to more efficient problem-solving, as team members can focus on the issue at hand rather than the emotional distractions that stress can cause. This clarity allows the team to collaborate more effectively and reach decisions faster. Ultimately, managing stress dynamics enhances communication by promoting transparency, understanding, and a calm approach to problem-solving.

Stronger Team Cohesion

Stress management is a key factor in fostering stronger team cohesion, as it allows team members to support each other during challenging times. High-performing teams that understand stress dynamics are more likely to exhibit empathy and consideration toward one another, recognizing that each person may experience and handle stress differently. This awareness helps prevent friction and promotes a more cooperative environment where members feel safe to express their concerns or seek help when needed. As team members practice stress-reducing techniques together, such as mindfulness or debriefing sessions after stressful events, they develop a stronger sense of camaraderie. Moreover, understanding stress allows team members to avoid blaming or scapegoating during high-pressure situations, focusing instead on collaborative solutions. When teams operate with this level of support, individuals are more likely to offer assistance to their peers, strengthening the bonds that keep the team united. This cohesive approach ensures that the team can weather difficult situations together without falling apart.

Team cohesion is further enhanced when stress management is embedded in the team's culture. High-performing teams that prioritize stress awareness create a supportive atmosphere where individuals can openly discuss the pressures they face and share strategies for coping. This openness fosters trust among team members, as they recognize that their colleagues will not only empathize with their struggles but also provide tangible support when necessary. In this type of environment, team members feel more connected and aligned with each other's goals, knowing that they are working together to achieve success. This shared experience of overcoming stressful situations strengthens the team's bond and builds a collective resilience that enhances performance. Ultimately, understanding the dynamics of stress reinforces team cohesion, creating a unified, high-functioning group capable of handling any challenge.

Improved Mental and Physical Well-Being

The ability to manage stress is vital for maintaining the mental and physical well-being of high-performing teams. Prolonged exposure to stress without effective coping mechanisms can lead to burnout, fatigue, and even serious health issues, such as anxiety, depression, or cardio-vascular problems. Teams that understand stress dynamics can take proactive measures to ensure that stress levels remain manageable and that members are equipped with the tools they need to protect their well-being. This might include promoting healthy work–life balance, encouraging regular breaks, and offering access to wellness resources, such as mental health support or physical activity programs. When teams prioritize well-being in this way, members are less likely to suffer from the negative effects of stress, which can lead to higher job satisfaction and reduced absenteeism. Additionally, managing stress effectively helps individuals maintain their focus and energy, enabling them to perform at their best over the long term.

Improving mental and physical well-being through stress management also contributes to a more sustainable work environment. High-performing teams that understand the dynamics of stress are more likely to identify signs of burnout early and intervene before it becomes a serious issue. This not only prevents health-related disruptions but also fosters a more positive and productive team culture. By promoting practices such as mindfulness, exercise, and self-care, teams can maintain high levels of energy and resilience, even during periods of intense work. Furthermore, addressing stress proactively reduces the likelihood of turnover, as employees are more likely to stay with organizations that prioritize their health and well-being. In the long run, teams that emphasize well-being can sustain high levels of performance without sacrificing the health of their members. Ultimately, understanding stress dynamics is crucial for maintaining both mental and physical well-being, ensuring the long-term success and sustainability of high-performing teams.

Conclusion

Understanding the dynamics of stress is a critical skill for high-performing teams, as it enhances communication, strengthens team cohesion, and improves overall well-being. By managing stress effectively, teams can avoid the common pitfalls of miscommunication, build stronger bonds of support and collaboration, and create a healthier, more sustainable work environment. Practicing these essential skills not only enables teams to perform at their best during high-pressure situations but also ensures their longevity and resilience in the face of challenges. As a recent study states, "high-performing teams that prioritize stress management are 40 percent more likely to maintain high productivity levels during stressful periods."[1] As teams continue to evolve and adapt to the demands of modern work, mastering stress dynamics will remain a key factor in achieving lasting success.

Self-Reflection Questions

1. How do I currently handle stress in high-pressure situations, and how does it impact my communication with others?

2. What are some common stressors in my team, and how can I contribute to better stress management practices?

3. In what ways can I improve my ability to listen actively and maintain emotional control during stressful conversations?

4. How do I approach conflicts in my team when stress levels are high, and what strategies can I use to resolve them constructively?

5. How can I foster stronger empathy and support among my team members to help manage stress collectively?

6. What practices can my team implement to promote stress awareness and encourage open discussions about challenges?

7. How do I balance my own stress levels while ensuring that I am contributing to a cohesive, supportive team dynamic?

8. What steps can I take to prioritize both my mental and physical well-being while maintaining high levels of performance?

9. How can my team better identify early signs of burnout and intervene before it affects our overall productivity?

10. What long-term strategies can I implement to ensure that stress management becomes an integral part of our team culture?

CHAPTER 23

Challenge Your Assumptions

Introduction

Challenging assumptions is an essential skill for high-performing teams as it allows them to push beyond conventional thinking and explore new possibilities. By regularly questioning long-held beliefs, teams foster a mindset that values diversity of thought, avoids the dangers of groupthink, and sparks creative innovation. As Jay Sullivan noted in *Forbes*: "to contribute most meaningfully at work, and to avoid the kinds of assumptions that keep us from being more successful, we need to challenge that most basic thinking."[1] These skills not only lead to better decision making but also enable teams to be more adaptable, inclusive, and innovative in their approach to problem-solving. Through this practice, teams can tap into a wealth of new perspectives and ideas that drive both individual and collective growth.

Promoting Diversity of Thought

Challenging assumptions plays a vital role in promoting diversity of thought within high-performing teams. When teams make a conscious effort to question their own biases and preconceptions, they open the door to a wider range of perspectives and ideas. This creates an environment where every team member's voice is valued, regardless of their background or experiences. By fostering an inclusive space for diverse viewpoints, teams can uncover insights that might otherwise be overlooked, leading to more well-rounded and creative solutions. This diversity of thought also helps to challenge the status quo, allowing teams to break free from conventional approaches and explore innovative strategies. Moreover, by embracing different perspectives, teams build a culture of collaboration, where members feel empowered to contribute their unique ideas without fear of judgment. As a result, the team benefits from a richer decision making process that draws on a wide array of viewpoints, ultimately leading to better outcomes.

Promoting diversity of thought is also essential for teams to remain competitive in today's complex, globalized world. Teams that challenge their assumptions are more likely to seek out diverse talent and viewpoints, recognizing that innovation often stems from the convergence of different ideas and perspectives. This diversity not only enhances the team's creativity but also helps them adapt to the needs of a diverse customer base or marketplace. By questioning their assumptions about how things "should" be done, teams become more flexible in their thinking and more open to unconventional approaches. In turn, this leads to greater innovation and a broader range of solutions to the challenges they face. Ultimately, challenging assumptions and promoting diversity of thought allows teams to remain agile and innovative in an ever-changing world, ensuring their long-term success.

Avoiding Groupthink

Avoiding groupthink is another critical reason why high-performing teams should challenge their assumptions. Groupthink occurs when team members prioritize consensus over critical thinking, leading to poor decision making and the suppression of alternative viewpoints. When teams challenge their assumptions, they encourage open dialogue and foster a culture of healthy debate, which helps to prevent groupthink from taking hold. By questioning established norms and inviting dissenting opinions, teams can evaluate ideas more rigorously and make better-informed decisions. This practice also reduces the risk of teams falling into patterns of conformity, where members may feel pressured to align with the majority opinion, even if they disagree. Challenging assumptions empowers team members to speak up when they have concerns, fostering a more democratic and inclusive decision making process. In doing so, teams can avoid the dangers of groupthink and ensure that all ideas are thoroughly evaluated before moving forward.

As part of this essential skill, teams that actively work to avoid groupthink by challenging assumptions are more likely to develop innovative solutions. When dissenting opinions are welcomed and assumptions are questioned, the team is more likely to uncover new perspectives that could lead to breakthroughs in their work. This critical evaluation of ideas ensures that decisions are made based on merit rather than conformity, reducing the likelihood of errors or overlooked opportunities. Moreover, challenging groupthink encourages continuous improvement, as teams regularly reassess their strategies and adapt them based on new information or changing circumstances. By avoiding groupthink, teams remain agile and adaptable, capable of responding effectively to new challenges and opportunities. Ultimately, this practice of questioning assumptions and encouraging diverse viewpoints leads to stronger, more resilient teams that are better equipped to succeed in complex environments.

Sparking Creative Thought

Challenging assumptions is also essential for sparking creative thought within high-performing teams. When team members are encouraged to question long-held beliefs, they are more likely to think outside the box and explore new ideas that break away from traditional approaches. This practice of challenging assumptions helps to disrupt ingrained patterns of thinking and opens the door to fresh, innovative solutions. By questioning what is considered "normal" or "expected," teams can discover new ways to approach problems that may not have been apparent before. Additionally, this process fosters a mindset of curiosity and exploration, where team members are constantly seeking to push boundaries and test new ideas. In doing so, teams become more creative in their approach to challenges, developing solutions that are not only effective but also original and forward-thinking.

Moreover, the act of challenging assumptions creates an environment that supports continuous creativity and innovation. High-performing teams that regularly question their assumptions cultivate a culture of experimentation, where team members feel encouraged to take risks and explore new possibilities without fear of failure. This leads to a more dynamic and creative problem-solving process, where ideas are tested, refined, and improved upon through open dialogue and collaboration. By fostering an environment where creativity is valued and assumptions are continuously challenged, teams can maintain a steady flow of innovative ideas that keep them ahead of the curve. Ultimately, challenging assumptions is a key driver of creative thought, enabling teams to think beyond the obvious and develop groundbreaking solutions that drive progress and success.

Conclusion

Challenging assumptions is a vital skill for high-performing teams, as it promotes diversity of thought, prevents groupthink, and sparks creative innovation. By questioning deeply held beliefs and encouraging open dialogue, teams can tap into a wealth of new ideas and perspectives that drive progress and growth. This practice not only leads to better decision making but also fosters a culture of collaboration, inclusion, and creativity. As teams continue to navigate the complexities of modern work, mastering the skill of challenging assumptions will be essential for staying competitive, innovative, and adaptable in the face of change. As with each of these essential skills, challenging and letting go of assumptions begins with a willingness to become more reflective, become willing to let go of our "rightness," and revisit the thoughts we are holding on to. Examining your own thoughts and beliefs is an act of courage. This in an of itself is hard to do. Remember, you can do hard things. Take time to reflect, be willing to let go of our "rightness," and revisit the thoughts we are holding on to. Examining your own thoughts and beliefs is an act of courage. allow yourself to recognize how wxamining your own thoughts and beliefs is an act of courage.

Self-Reflection Questions

1. How often do I challenge my own assumptions or question deeply held beliefs in my team's decision making process?
2. In what ways have I fostered an environment that encourages diverse perspectives and values every team member's input?

3. How can I become more open to exploring unconventional approaches to problem-solving?

4. What steps can I take to prevent groupthink in my team and ensure that all viewpoints are considered before reaching a consensus?

5. How do I respond when a team member challenges my assumptions or offers a dissenting opinion?

6. What strategies can I use to promote continuous creativity and experimentation within my team?

7. How well does my team adapt to changing circumstances, and how can questioning assumptions improve our adaptability?

8. How can I encourage a mindset of curiosity and exploration in my team to spark innovative solutions?

9. What role do diverse viewpoints play in my team's current decision making process, and how can I ensure that they are more deeply integrated?

10. How can challenging my own assumptions help me grow as a leader and contribute to the overall success of my team?

CHAPTER 24

Leverage the Two Dimensions of Time

Introduction

High-performing teams must effectively balance the two dimensions of time—chronos (linear, measurable time) and kairos (opportune, qualitative time)—to succeed in today's dynamic work environments. Chronos represents the structured aspect of time, allowing teams to meet deadlines and maintain productivity, while kairos focuses on recognizing the right moments to act for maximum impact. Understanding and leveraging these dimensions enables teams to allocate resources effectively, manage risks more strategically, and optimize overall performance. While chronos ensures that teams stay on track, kairos allows them to seize opportunities that lead to breakthroughs. As Dan Ryan observed, "one of the key ingredients that great leaders have is their ability to utilize either Chronos or Kairos skills when the situation presents itself."[1] By mastering both dimensions, high-performing teams can manage their short-term tasks efficiently while positioning themselves for long-term success and adaptability.

Improved Resource Allocation

Effective resource allocation requires balancing chronos and kairos. Chronos allows teams to distribute resources according to a predefined timeline, ensuring that tasks are completed on time and with minimal waste. This structured approach helps teams maintain efficiency and ensure that resources are used appropriately for routine tasks and projects. However, if a team focuses solely on chronos, they may miss out on unexpected opportunities. Kairos comes into play by encouraging teams to recognize when a unique moment arises, requiring a reallocation of resources to maximize impact. For instance, when a high-value client suddenly becomes available or a new market opens up, kairos empowers teams to adapt quickly and seize that moment. Balancing these dimensions allows teams to be both disciplined and flexible, ensuring that they are methodical in their planning but adaptive when conditions shift unexpectedly. Ultimately, mastering both chronos and kairos leads to more efficient resource management and heightened innovation.

Incorporating kairos alongside chronos increases a team's ability to respond to immediate demands while remaining agile. Teams that recognize the importance of kairos can shift resources at the right time to address unforeseen challenges or opportunities, ensuring that they are not locked into rigid schedules. This balance ensures that teams meet their planned goals while remaining ready to capitalize on new developments. By utilizing chronos to maintain order and kairos to stay responsive, teams can optimize their resources for maximum efficiency and innovation. This dual approach makes high-performing teams more adaptable, giving them the ability to pivot effectively while maintaining their overall strategic objectives.

Better Risk Management

Leveraging chronos and kairos also enhances a team's risk management capabilities. Chronos ensures that progress is monitored, deadlines are met, and resources are used effectively, which reduces the risks of project delays or misalignment with goals. With this structure in place, teams can track potential risks early and take proactive measures to address them. However, successful risk management requires more than just following a timeline—it involves understanding the right moments to act, which is where kairos plays a key role. Kairos enables teams to assess when to take calculated risks based on timing and opportunity. For example, launching a new product at the right time could be a crucial factor in its success. By balancing chronos and kairos, teams make more informed decisions about when to take risks and when to wait, minimizing potential downsides while maximizing gains.

Kairos also helps teams identify moments that reduce risk, such as delaying a project until more data is available or waiting for the market to shift in their favor. Teams skilled in kairos can recognize when circumstances align for risk-taking, allowing them to capitalize on favorable conditions. This strategic timing reduces the likelihood of poor decision making driven by urgency and ensures that risks are carefully calculated based on both chronological progress and situational awareness. Teams that effectively combine the discipline of chronos with the flexibility of kairos are better equipped to handle uncertainties and navigate complex environments. Ultimately, this balanced approach to risk management allows teams to operate with both stability and growth in mind.

Optimized Team Performance

High-performing teams achieve optimized performance by balancing the structure of chronos with the strategic timing of kairos. Chronos allows teams to meet deadlines, maintain steady workflows, and ensure that projects are completed on time. This consistency is vital for building momentum and achieving short-term goals. However, focusing solely on chronos can lead to missed opportunities for creativity and breakthroughs. Kairos adds the dimension of recognizing the right moments for innovation, reflection, or change, allowing teams to pause when necessary and act with maximum impact when the timing is ideal. By mastering both chronos and kairos, teams can maintain high productivity levels while also being strategic about when to push forward and when to step back.

Kairos also encourages reflection and strategic decision making, helping teams avoid the constant pressure of urgency. Teams that recognize kairos know how to balance quality and timing, ensuring that they are not simply working fast but also working smart. This balance allows them to prioritize quality and creativity, ensuring that their work is not just done on time but also makes a meaningful impact. By managing their energy and focus in this way, teams prevent burnout and maximize their effectiveness during key moments. Ultimately, leveraging both chronos and kairos enables high-performing teams to sustain their performance over the long term, blending timely execution with strategic innovation for sustained excellence.

Conclusion

Leveraging both chronos and kairos empowers high-performing teams to improve resource allocation, enhance risk management, and optimize overall performance. Recognizing the value of structured timelines (chronos) and seizing opportune moments (kairos) allows teams to balance efficiency with adaptability, ensuring that they remain competitive in today's fast-paced environments. This dual approach equips teams with the flexibility to make strategic decisions, manage risks effectively, and optimize their performance both in routine tasks and critical moments. As work environments continue to evolve, mastering the balance between chronos and kairos will be a crucial skill for teams striving for long-term success and resilience.

Self-Reflection Questions

1. How well do I understand the difference between chronos and kairos in my work?
2. Do I focus more on meeting deadlines (chronos) or seizing opportunities (kairos)? How can I balance both?
3. How does my team currently allocate resources, and are we flexible enough to adapt to unexpected opportunities?
4. In what ways could I improve my ability to recognize key moments (kairos) for acting or making decisions?
5. How does our current approach to risk management account for both planned timelines and opportune moments?
6. Are there instances where my team has missed opportunities because we were too focused on sticking to a timeline?
7. How can I encourage my team to be more adaptable in reallocating resources when unexpected opportunities arise?

8. What steps can I take to balance productivity (chronos) with strategic decision making (kairos) in my daily tasks?
9. How do I ensure that my team takes time to reflect on the best moments to innovate or take action?
10. How can leveraging both chronos and kairos contribute to my team's long-term success and sustainability?

Conclusion—The Nuance of Essential Skills

According to the World Economic Forum Future of Jobs Report published in January 2025, employers and employees around the world can expect "significant ongoing skills disruption with employers expecting 39% of workers' core skills to change by 2030."[1]

It is crucial for leaders of high-performing teams to understand nuance because it enables them to guide their teams with a deeper awareness of the subtle differences between similar but distinct attributes. Leaders who recognize nuance can tailor their approaches, fostering environments where diverse perspectives, skills, and growth mechanisms thrive. This capacity to distinguish between overlapping ideas is especially important in guiding teams toward innovation, resilience, and productivity. Nuance allows leaders to address individual needs, make strategic decisions, and cultivate a team dynamic that balances both creativity and structure. By understanding the fine details, leaders can avoid blanket solutions and instead apply targeted strategies that enhance team performance. Specifically, in terms of encouraging experimentation and learning from failures versus learning from failure and iterating on ideas, the difference lies in fostering a mindset of risk-taking and experimentation versus focusing on refining ideas through a structured, continuous learning process. While both emphasize learning from failure, understanding the nuance allows leaders to know when to push for creative risk-taking and when to encourage iterative improvements based on feedback.

Similarly, the distinction between promoting diversity of thought and inclusion and promoting diversity of thought and avoiding groupthink is essential. Inclusion is about ensuring that every voice is heard and represented, creating a welcoming environment for diverse perspectives. Avoiding groupthink, on the other hand, focuses on intellectual rigor and preventing consensus-based decision making that stifles innovation. A leader who grasps this nuance can promote a culture that values representation while also challenging team members to think independently and push boundaries. In the case of fostering work–life balance and healthy boundaries versus encouraging healthy habits and practices, the former focuses on setting clear external boundaries between work and personal life, while the latter encourages ongoing internal behaviors that contribute to long-term well-being. Leaders need to know when to implement policies that protect personal time and when to encourage habits that enhance daily resilience.

The difference between providing opportunities for feedback and self-assessment and fostering an environment of honesty and transparency in self-evaluation lies in the formality and structure of feedback mechanisms versus fostering a continuous culture of candid reflection. Understanding this nuance allows leaders to build systems that support growth while nurturing an environment where honesty and transparency are valued on an ongoing basis. For fostering a sense of purpose and direction within the team versus helping team members develop a strong personal identity, leaders must balance aligning the team with a shared vision while simultaneously supporting individual growth. This nuanced understanding helps leaders ensure that both team cohesion and personal fulfillment are achieved, driving collective success and personal satisfaction.

In navigating ambiguity, the difference between creating opportunities from ambiguity and leveraging fortuitous events for growth is critical. The former is proactive, encouraging teams to extract potential from uncertain situations, while the latter is reactive, capitalizing on unexpected opportunities. Leaders who understand this nuance can guide their teams to be both innovative in uncertain times and agile in responding to chance events. The contrast between fostering a culture of focus and attention to the task at hand and promoting awareness of the here and now to maximize productivity, lies in focus-driven task completion versus a broader mindfulness that enhances overall presence and clarity. Leaders can foster productivity by knowing when to emphasize concentrated effort and when to encourage a more holistic awareness that promotes mental clarity across tasks.

In terms of mindfulness, encouraging mindfulness and presence in day-to-day activities versus promoting mindfulness practices and techniques for managing emotions requires leaders to distinguish between promoting overall engagement in daily activities and using mindfulness as a tool for emotional regulation. Understanding this difference helps leaders enhance both productivity and emotional well-being within their teams. Finally, recognizing the impact of stress on performance versus creating strategies for managing stress effectively highlights the importance of recognizing the effects of stress and providing actionable tools for coping with it. Leaders who grasp this distinction can create both awareness and practical solutions, ensuring that stress is managed effectively for sustained high performance.

Notes

Introduction

1. Rossingol, *RUNN*.
2. Madhosingh, *Forbes*.
3. Harter, Gallup.
4. Witters and Bayne, Gallup.
5. Ibid.
6. Dickler, *CNBC News*.
7. State of the Global Workplace: 2023 Report.
8. Harter, Gallup.
9. Ibid.
10. State of the Global Workplace: 2023 Report.

Defining Essential Skills

1. 2024 LinkedIn Workplace Learning Report.
2. Kratz, *Forbes*.
3. De Marco, Fast Company.
4. Deloitte Insights, "2024 Global Human Capital Trends."
5. Kratz, *Forbes*.
6. "Leadership Often Hinges on Team-Building Skills." *The Wall Street Journal*.

Chapter 1

1. Channel Futures, "A Growth Mindset: Your Organization's Strategic Differentiator."
2. Ibid.
3. Sher, *Forbes*.
4. Winstead, "Fostering a Culture of Continuous Learning in the Workplace."
5. McKenna, "Build a Strong Learning Culture on Your Team."
6. Ibid.
7. Gardiner, "Psychological Safety & Positive Psychology: A Leadership Guide."

Chapter 2

1. Reeves and Deimler, "Adaptability: The New Competitive Advantage."
2. Perry, "Supply Chain 2024: Why the Pace of Change Will AcceleraZte."
3. Reeves and Deimler, "Adaptability: The New Competitive Advantage."
4. McKinsey, "The Social Economy: Unlocking Value and Productivity Through Social Technologies."
5. Linkedin, "Statistics on Why Effective Communication Is Important in the Workplace."
6. Center for Creative Leadership, "Build High-Performing Teams With Our Team Effectiveness Framework."
7. Wachter, "The Importance of Embracing Change in Business."

Chapter 3

1. Meyer, "Here's Why You Should Encourage Employees To Write To Their Future Selves."
2. Satell and Windschitl, "High-Performing Teams Start With A Culture of Shared Values."
3. https://jamesclear.com/quotes/you-do-not-rise-to-the-level-of-your-goals-you-fall-to-the-level-of-your-systems.
4. Kozlowski and Ilgen, "Enhancing the Effectiveness of Work Groups and Teams," 77–124.
5. Lundberg, "Managing Through Uncertainty."
6. Jeifetz, "Maximizing Organization Success Through Team Effectiveness."
7. Kilduff and West, "The One Personality Trait Crucial to Creating Effective Teams."
8. "20 Effective Ways To Build A More Resilient Team," *Forbes*.

Chapter 4

1. Shenker, "E.B. White: Notes and Comment by Author."
2. Smith, "Digital Transformation Success Starts With Leadership at the Top."
3. Ibid.
4. https://jamesclear.com/quotes/you-do-not-rise-to-the-level-of-your-goals-you-fall-to-the-level-of-your-systems

5. Newport, "Deep Work: Rules for Focused Success in a Distracted World."

6. Brooks, "The Quiet Magic of Middle Managers."

7. Ibid.

Chapter 5

1. Teti, "Building Grit in Teams: A Blueprint for Leadership."

2. Rainey, "Building Resilience in the Workplace: Strategies for Success."

3. Kininmonth, "Why Worklife Adam Grant's Take on Psychological Safety Is Timely for Australian."

4. Ibid.

5. Intrafocus, "Resilient high-performing teams," Intrafocus, June 1, 2023.

Chapter 6

1. Eurich, "Insight: The Surprising Truth About How Others See Us, How We See Ourselves, and Why the Answers Matter More Than We Think."

2. StandfordReport, "Jobs."

3. https://holdingarealactualbook.wordpress.com/2014/12/05/chapter-41-on-becoming-a-person-by-carl-rogers/

4. Verywellmind, "Self-Efficacy and Why Believing in Yourself Matters."

Chapter 7

1. Lauren, et al., "To Retain Employees, Support Their Passions Outside Work."

2. Ibid.

3. Burns, "The Importance of Cultivating A Passion Outside of Work."

Chapter 8

1. Laker, "Patience Unveiled: A Superpower for Personal Growth and Harmony."

2. Shellenbarger, "Are You Agile Enough for Agile Management."

3. Ibid.

4. Stobierski, "The Advantages of Data-Driven Decision-Making."

5. Ibid.

6. David, "5 Reasons Why Persistent Leaders Lead Best."

Chapter 9

1. Zucker and Rowell, "6 Strategies for Leading Through Uncertainty."

2. Wartzman and Tang, "The Key to Being a Successful Leader? It's Adaptability."

3. Lehnig, LinkedIn.

4. Zucker and Rowell, "6 Strategies for Leading Through Uncertainty."

5. Acar, Tarakci, and van Knippenberg, "Why Constraints Are Good for Innovation."

6. Wartzman and Tang, "The Key to Being a Successful Leader? It's Adaptability."

Chapter 10

1. Cernega, et al., "Volatility, Uncertainty, Complexity, and Ambiguity (VUCA) in Healthcare." 773.

2. Ibid.

3. Natale, Poppensieker, and Thun, "From risk management to strategic resilience."

4. Haryanto, "Thinking Outside the Box: Unconventional Approaches to Innovation."

5. Henley, "The VUCA World Is Now—Here's How to Face It."

Chapter 11

1. Amazon Leadership Principles.

2. "Creating a Culture of Experimentation."

3. Landry, "Why Managers Should Involve Their Team in the Decision-Making Process."

4. Dewar, "How Continuous Improvement Can Build a Competitive Edge."

Chapter 12

1. Landry, "Why Managers Should Involve Their Team in the Decision-Making Process."
2. Eikenberry," Groupthink and Teamthink."
3. Reynolds and Lewis, "Teams Solve Problems Faster When They're More Cognitively Diverse.
4. Aggarwal, et al., "The Impact of Cognitive Style Diversity on Impliit Learning in Teams." 112.
5. Dreifus, "In Professor's Model, Diversity—Productivity."
6. Danao, "11 Essential Soft Skills In 2024 (With Examples)."
7. Facione, "Critical Thinking: What It Is and Why It Counts."

Chapter 13

1. Kolzow, "Leading From Within: Building Organizational Leadership Capacity."
2. Webb, "Bringing True Strategic Foresight Back to Business."

Chapter 14

1. Lencioni, "The Most Important Leadership Trait You Shun."
2. Gleeson, "4 Ways to Lead With Humility and Vulnerability in High-Performance Teams."

Chapter 15

1. Silverman, "The Science o Serendipity in the Workplace."
2. Chen, "Virtual Meetings Are Killing the Vibe. Here's What to Do About It."
3. Johansson, "When Success Is Born Out of Serendipity."

Chapter 16

1. Evans, "Psychological Safety: Building High-Performing Teams."

Chapter 17

1. Sokoler, "The Business Care for Mental Health: Investing in Employee Well-Being."
2. 2023 Work in America Survey, American Psychological Association.
3. Ibid.
4. Wong and Greenwood, "The Future of Mental Health at Work Is Safety, Community, and a Healthy Organizational Culture."
5. Ibid.
6. Sokoler, "The Business Care for Mental Health: Investing in Employee Well-Being."

Chapter 18

1. Bernhard, Psychology Today.
2. McKinsey & Company, "How to Demonstrate Calm and Optimism in a Crisis."
3. Yu and Zellmer-Bruhn, *Harvard Business Review*
4. Ibid.
5. Swift, *MIT Sloan Management Review*.
6. Ibid.
7. Capgemini Research Institute, "Emotional Intelligence-the Essential Skill-set for the Age of AI."
8. Ibid.

Chapter 19

1. Newport, "Deep Work: Rules for Focused Success in a Distracted World."
2. "Mindfulness and Productivity: Strategies to Enhance Focus and Efficiency in the Workplace."

Chapter 20

1. Gallup, "State of the Global Workplace."
2. Gallup, "Employee Wellbeing."

Chapter 21

1. Barnhill, *Forbes.*

Chapter 22

1. Cainey, *HR Magazine.*

Chapter 23

1. Sullivan, *Forbes.*

Chapter 24

1. Ryan, LinkedIn.

Conclusion

1. World Economic Forum, Future of Jobs Report, 2025. https://www.weforum.org/publications/the-future-of-jobs-report-2025/

References

"20 Effective Ways to Build a More Resilient Team." *Forbes*, March 6, 2024. www.forbes.com/sites/forbescoachescouncil/2024/03/06/20-effective-ways-to-build-a-more-resilient-team/.

"Build High-Performing Teams With Our Team Effectiveness Framework." *CCL*. October 22, 2023. www.ccl.org/articles/leading-effectively-articles/building-high-performing-teams-with-our-team-effectiveness-framework/.

"Leadership Often Hinges on Team-Building Skills." *The Wall Street Journal*. May 4, 2021. https://deloitte.wsj.com/riskandcompliance/leadership-often-hinges-on-team-building-skills-01620154930.

Acar, O.A., M. Tarakci, and D. van Knippenberg. 2019. "Why Constraints Are Good for Innovation." *Harvard Business Review*, November 22. https://hbr.org/2019/11/why-constraints-are-good-for-innovation.

Aggarwal I, A.W. Woolley, C.F. Chabris, and T.W. Malone. February 7, 2019. "The Impact of Cognitive Style Diversity on Implicit Learning in Teams." *Front Psychol* 10: 112. doi: 10.3389/fpsyg.2019.00112. PMID: 30792672; PMCID: PMC6374291.

Amazon Jobs. n.d. "Amazon Leadership Principles." www.amazon.jobs/content/en/our-workplace/leadership-principles.

American Psychological Association. n.d. "2023 Work in America Survey, American Psychological Association." www.apa.org/pubs/reports/work-in-america/2023-workplace-health-well-being.

Barnhill, A. 2024. "The House of Empathy: Cultivating High-Performing Teams and Organizational Excellence." *Forbes*, July 2. www.forbes.com/councils/forbescoachescouncil/2024/07/02/the-house-of-empathy-cultivating-high-performing-teams-and-organizational-excellence/.

Bernhard, T. 2019. "Equanimity: The Key to Happiness." *Psychology Today*, November 7. www.psychologytoday.com/us/blog/turning-straw-gold/201911/equanimity-the-key-happiness.

Brooks, D. 2024. "The Quiet Magic of Middle Managers." *The New York Times*, April 11. www.nytimes.com/2024/04/11/opinion/middle-managers-business-society.html.

Burns, S. 2020. "The Importance of Cultivating A Passion Outside of Work." *Forbes*, March 7. www.forbes.com/sites/stephanieburns/2020/03/07/the-importance-of-cultivating-a-passion-outside-of-work/.

Cainey, J. 2020. "In Uncertain Times We Need to Raise the Benchmark." *HR Magazine*, December 8. www.hrmagazine.co.uk/content/features/in-uncertain-times-we-need-to-raise-the-benchmark/#:~:text=What's%20 more%2C%20according%20to%20the,attention%20to%20their%20 employee%20engagement.

Capgemini Research Institute. n.d. "Emotional Intelligence-the Essential Skillset for the Age of AI." www.capgemini.com/gb-en/wp-content/uploads/ sites/3/2019/10/Digital-Report–Emotional-Intelligence.pdf.

Cernega A, D.N. Nicolescu, M. Meleşcanu-Imre, A.R. Totan, A.L. Arsene, R.S. Şerban, A.C. Perpelea et al. April 2, 2024. "Volatility, Uncertainty, Complexity, and Ambiguity (VUCA) in Healthcare." *Healthcare (Basel)* 12 (7):773. doi: 10.3390/healthcare12070773. PMID: 38610195; PMCID: PMC11011466.

Channel Futures. 2022. "A Growth Mindset: Your Organization's Strategic Differentiator." August 1. www.channelfutures.com/channel-sales-marketing/ a-growth-mindset-your-organization-s-strategic-differentiator.

Chen, T-P. 2024. "Virtual Meetings Are Killing the Vibe. Here's What to Do About It." *The Wall Street Journal*, February 29. www.wsj.com/lifestyle/ workplace/hybrid-work-jobs-company-culture-6b1cb6e7.

Danao, M. 2024. "11 Essential Soft Skills in 2024 (With Examples)." *Forbes*, April 28. www.forbes.com/advisor/business/soft-skills-examples/.

David, R. 2023. "5 Reasons Why Persistent Leaders Lead Best." *SHRM*, August 10. www.shrm.org/executive-network/insights/5-reasons-persistent-leaders-lead-best.

De Marco, N. 2024. "Soft Skills Are Dead, Long Live 'Skills.'" *Fast Company*, September 13. www.fastcompany.com/91190404/soft-skills-are-dead-long-live-skills.

Delloite. n.d. "Creating a Culture of Experimentation." https://deloitte.wsj.com/ cmo/creating-a-culture-of-experimentation-1478145752.

Deloitte Insights. n.d. "2024 Global Human Capital Trends." www2.deloitte. com/us/en/insights/focus/human-capital-trends.html/#navigating-the-end.

Dewar, D. 2019. "How Continuous Improvement Can Build a Competitive Edge." *McKinsey*, May 6. www.mckinsey.com/capabilities/people-and-organizational-performance/our-insights/the-organization-blog/how-continuous-improvement-can-build-a-competitive-edge.

Dickler, J. 2023. "62% of Americans Are Still Living Paycheck to Paycheck, Making It 'the Main Financial Lifestyle.' Report Finds." *CNBC News*, October 31. www.cnbc.com/2023/10/31/62percent-of-americans-still-live-paycheck-to-paycheck-amid-inflation.html#:~:text=High%20inflation%20 and%20higher%20interest,is%20unchanged%20from%20last%20year; PYMNTS. 2023. "New Reality Check: The Paycheck-to-Paycheck Report." November. www.pymnts.com/study/reality-check-paycheck-to-paycheck-holiday-shopping-credit-financing/.

Dreifus, C. 2008. "In Professor's Model, Diversity—Productivity." *The New York Times*, January 8. www.nytimes.com/2008/01/08/science/08conv.html.

Eikenberry, K. 2015. "Groupthink and Teamthink." *LinkedIn*, December 14. www.linkedin.com/pulse/whats-difference-between-groupthink-teamthink-kevin-eikenberry/.

Eurich, T. 2018. *Insight: The Surprising Truth About How Others See Us, How We See Ourselves, and Why the Answers Matter More Than We Think*. https://tinyurl.com/xjzbv2n2.

Evans, M. 2022. "Psychological Safety: Building High-Performing Teams." *Forbes*, October 12. www.forbes.com/councils/forbesbusinesscouncil/2022/10/12/psychological-safety-building-high-performing-teams/.

Facione, P. 2015. "Critical Thinking: What It Is and Why It Counts." *Insight Assessment*, January. www.researchgate.net/publication/251303244_Critical_Thinking_What_It_Is_and_Why_It_Counts.

Gallup. 2023. "State of the Global Workplace." www.gallup.com/workplace/349484/state-of-the-global-workplace.aspx.

Gallup. n.d. "Employee Wellbeing." www.gallup.com/394424/indicator-employee-wellbeing.aspx.

Gallup. n.d. "State of the Global Workplace: 2023 Report." www.gallup.com/workplace/349484/state-of-the-global-workplace.aspx#ite-506891.

Gardiner, K. 2023. "Psychological Safety & Positive Psychology: A Leadership Guide." *Positive Psychology*, September 21. https://positivepsychology.com/psychological-safety/#:~:text=Psychological%20safety%20is%20the%20bedrock,cultural%20behaviors%20they%20themselves%20model.

Gleeson, B. 2023. "4 Ways to Lead With Humility and Vulnerability in High-Performance Teams." *Forbes*, October 10. www.forbes.com/sites/brentgleeson/2023/10/10/the-4-ways-to-lead-with-humility-and-vulnerability-in-high-performance-teams/.

Harter, J. 2024. "In New Workplace, U.S. Employee Engagement Stagnates." Gallup, January 23. www.gallup.com/workplace/608675/new-workplace-employee-engagement-stagnates.aspx.

Harter, J. September 4, 2024. "World Largest Ongoing Study of the Employee Experience." Gallup. www.gallup.com/workplace/649487/world-largest-ongoing-study-employee-experience.aspx?utm_source=gallup_brand&utm_medium=email&utm_campaign=gallup_at_work_september_1_09102024&utm_term=information&utm_content=image_imagelink_1.

Haryanto, B. 2023. "Thinking Outside the Box: Unconventional Approaches to Innovation." *LinkedIn*, July 6. www.linkedin.com/pulse/thinking-outside-box-unconventional-approaches-bambang-haryanto/.

Henley, D. 2024. "The VUCA World Is Now–Here's How to Face It." *Forbes*, May 19. www.forbes.com/sites/dedehenley/2024/05/19/the-vuca-world-is-now-heres-how-to-face-it/.

Howe, L.C., J.M. Jachimowicz, and J.I. Menges, "To Retain Employees, Support Their Passions Outside Work." *Harvard Business Review*, March 30. https://hbr.org/2022/03/to-retain-employees-support-their-passions-outside-work

Intrafocus. 2023. "Resilient High-Performing Teams." June 1. www.intrafocus.com/2023/06/resilient-high-performing-teams/.

Jeifetz, M. 2024. "Maximizing Organization Success Through Team Effectiveness." *Forbes*. www.forbes.com/sites/forbescoachescouncil/2024/02/06/maximizing-organization-success-through-team-effectiveness/.

Jobs, S. 2005. June 12. https://news.stanford.edu/stories/2005/06/youve-got-find-love-jobs-says.

Johansson, F. 2012. "When Success Is Born Out of Serendipity." *Harvard Business Review*, October 19. https://hbr.org/2012/10/when-success-is-born-out-of-serendipity.

Kilduff, G., and T. West. 2023. "The One Personality Trait Crucial to Creating Effective Teams." *The Wall Street Journal*, February 12. www.wsj.com/articles/personality-managers-effective-teams-11675879509.

Kininmonth, C. 2023. "Why Worklife Adam Grant's Take on Psychological Safety Is Timely for Australian." *Growth Faculty*, August 22. https://thegrowthfaculty.com/articles/adamgrantpsychologicalsafety.

Kolzow, D.R. 2014. "Leading From Within: Building Organizational Leadership Capacity." *IEDC*. www.iedconline.org/clientuploads/Downloads/edrp/Leading_from_Within.pdf.

Kozlowski, S.W.J., and D.R. Ilgen. 2006. "Enhancing the Effectiveness of Work Groups and Teams." *Psychological Science in the Public Interest 7* (3): 77–124. https://doi.org/10.1111/j.1529-1006.2006.00030.x.

Kratz, J. 2023. "The Rise of AI Underscore A Need for Human Skills." *Forbes*, December 17. www.forbes.com/sites/juliekratz/2023/12/17/have-we-forgotten-about-human-skills-in-the-age-of-ai/?sh=75b354666a7d.

Laker, B. 2024. "Patience Unveiled: A Superpower for Personal Growth and Harmony." *Forbes*, January 24. www.forbes.com/sites/benjaminlaker/2024/01/24/patience-unveiled-a-superpower-for-personal-growth-and-harmony/.

Landry, L. 2020. "Why Managers Should Involve Their Team in the Decision-Making Process." *Harvard Business School*, March 5. https://online.hbs.edu/blog/post/team-decision-making.

Lehnig, M. 2024. "Resilience Unleashed: Thriving in A World of Change and Uncertainty." *LinkedIn*, Marcy 5. www.linkedin.com/pulse/resilience-unleashed-thriving-world-change-mathew-lehnig-f6gwc/.

Lencioni, P. 2010. "The Most Important Leadership Trait You Shun." *The Wall Street Journal*, June 22. www.wsj.com/articles/SB10001424052748704895204575321380627619388.

Linkedin. 2022. "Statistics on Why Effective Communication Is Important in the Workplace." June 20. www.linkedin.com/pulse/statistics-why-effective-communication-important-/.

LinkedIn. n.d. "2024 LinkedIn Workplace Learning Report." https://learning.linkedin.com/resources/workplace-learning-report.

Lundberg, A. 2022. "Managing Through Uncertainty." *MIT Sloan Management Review*, September 13. https://sloanreview.mit.edu/article/managing-through-uncertainty/.

Madhosingh, S. December 31, 2023. "How Savvy Leaders Drive Employee Productivity Ini or Out of the Office." *Forbes*. www.forbes.com/sites/drsamanthamadhosingh/2023/12/31/how-savvy-leaders-drive-employee-productivity-in-or-out-of-the-office/?sh=5aa762cd5ff9.

McKenna, J. 2023. "Build a Strong Learning Culture on Your Team." *Harvard Business Review*, June 6. https://hbr.org/2023/06/build-a-strong-learning-culture-on-your-team.

McKinsey & Company. 2020. "How to Demonstrate Calm and Optimism in a Crisis." April 30. www.mckinsey.com/capabilities/people-and-organizational-performance/our-insights/how-to-demonstrate-calm-and-optimism-in-a-crisis.

McKinsey. 2012. "The Social Economy: Unlocking Value and Productivity Through Social Technologies," July. www.mckinsey.com/industries/technology-media-and-telecommunications/our-insights/the-social-economy.

Meyer, J. 2020. "Here's Why You Should Encourage Employees to Write to Their Future Selves." *Forbes*, January 16. www.forbes.com/sites/ellevate/2020/01/16/heres-why-you-should-encourage-employees-to-write-to-their-future-selves/.

Natale, A., T. Poppensieker, and M. Thun. 2022. "From Risk Management to Strategic Resilience." McKinsey, March 9. www.mckinsey.com/capabilities/risk-and-resilience/our-insights/from-risk-management-to-strategic-resilience.

Newport, C. 2016. "Deep Work: Rules for Focused Success in a Distracted World." Amazon. www.amazon.com/gp/product/1455586692/ref=as_li_tl?ie=UTF8&camp=1789&creative=9325&creativeASIN=1455586692&linkCode=as2&tag=becomingbet0d-20&linkId=17a74f5671a25234e7fd3ba28c7bf52e.

Perry, N. 2023. "Supply Chain 2024: Why the Pace of Change Will Accelerate." *SupplyChain*, December 21. https://supplychaindigital.com/articles/supply-chain-2024-why-the-pace-of-change-will-accelerate.

Rainey, C. 2023. "Building Resilience in the Workplace: Strategies for Success." *Forbes*, July 11. www.forbes.com/sites/forbescoachescouncil/2023/07/11/building-resilience-in-the-workplace-strategies-for-success/.

Reeves, M., and M. Deimler. 2011. "Adaptability: The New Competitive Advantage." *Harvard Business Review*, July–August. https://hbr.org/2011/07/adaptability-the-new-competitive-advantage.

Reynolds, A., and D. Lewis. 2017. "Teams Solve Problems Faster When They're More Cognitively Diverse." *Harvard Business Review*, March 30. https://hbr.org/2017/03/teams-solve-problems-faster-when-theyre-more-cognitively-diverse.

Rossingol, N. January 3, 2024. "13 Ways to Enhance Productivity at Work." *RUNN*. www.runn.io/blog/how-to-be-more-productive.

Ryan, D. 2014. "Chronos Leaders and Kairos Leaders-Core Competencies," *LinkedIn*, December 4. www.linkedin.com/pulse/20141204140334-2054214-chronos-leaders-and-kairos-leaders-core-competencies/.

Satell, G., and C. Windschitl. 2021. "High-Performing Teams Start With a Culture of Shared Values." *Harvard Business Review*, May 11. https://hbr.org/2021/05/high-performing-teams-start-with-a-culture-of-shared-values.

Shellenbarger, S. 2019. "Are You Agile Enough for Agile Management." *The Wall Street Journal*, August 12. www.wsj.com/articles/are-you-agile-enough-for-agile-management-11565607600.

Shenker, I. 1969. "E.B. White: Notes and Comment by Author." *The New York Times*, July 11. https://archive.nytimes.com, www.nytimes.com/books/97/08/03/lifetimes/white-notes.html?_r=3.

Sher, R. 2022. "The Secret Of High-Performing Teams: Coherent Planning, Alignment And Execution." *Forbes*, February 23. www.forbes.com/sites/robertsher/2022/02/22/the-secret-of-high-performing-teams-coherent-planning-alignment-and-execution/?sh=1798f75433e8.

Silverman, R.E. 2013. "The Science of Serendipity in the Workplace." *The Wall Street Journal*, April 30. www.wsj.com/articles/SB10001424127887323798104578455081218505870.

Smith, T. 2023. "Digital Transformation Success Starts With Leadership at the Top." *The Wall Street Journal*, April 3. https://deloitte.wsj.com/cfo/digital-transformation-success-starts-with-leadership-at-the-top-be13b3a5.

Sokoler, S. 2024. "The Business Care for Mental Health: Investing in Employee Well-Being." *Forbes*, July 30. www.forbes.com/councils/forbesbusinesscouncil/2024/07/30/the-business-case-for-mental-health-investing-in-employee-well-being/#:~:text=Companies%20that%20prioritize%20mental%20well,that%20drives%20long-term%20success.

Stobierski, T. 2019. "The Advantages of Data-Driven Decision-Making." *Harvard Business School Online*, August 26. https://online.hbs.edu/blog/post/data-driven-decision-making.

Sullivan, J. 2024. "Improve Your Critical Thinking by Avoiding Assumptions," Forbes, April 25, 2024. https://www.forbes.com/sites/jaysullivan/2024/04/25/improve-your-critical-thinking-by-avoiding-assumptions/.

Swift, M. 2024. "Warm Hearts, Cold Reality: How to Build Team Empathy." *MIT Sloan Management Review*, February 27. https://sloanreview.mit.edu/article/warm-hearts-cold-reality-how-to-build-team-empathy/.

Teti, M. 2024. "Building Grit in Teams: A Blueprint for Leadership." *Fast Company*, January 8. www.fastcompany.com/91005865/building-grit-in-teams-a-blueprint-for-leadership.

Verywellmind. 2024. "Self-Efficacy and Why Believing in Yourself Matters." June 25. www.verywellmind.com/what-is-self-efficacy-2795954#:~:text=Albert%20Bandura%20defined%20self-efficacy,succeed%20in%20a%20particular%20situation.

Vorecol. n.d. "Mindfulness and Productivity: Strategies to Enhance Focus and Efficiency in the Workplace." https://psico-smart.com/en/blogs/blog-mindfulness-and-productivity-strategies-to-enhance-focus-and-efficiency-in-the-workplace-169078.

Wachter, C. 2023. "The Importance of Embracing Change in Business." Forbes, April 13. www.forbes.com/sites/forbesbusinesscouncil/2023/04/13/the-importance-of-embracing-change-in-business/?sh=6e59956c8268.

Wartzman, R. and K. Tang. 2023. "The Key to Being a Successful Leader? It's Adaptability." *The Wall Street Journal*, March 26. www.wsj.com/articles/the-key-to-being-a-successful-leader-its-adaptability-11585242768.

Webb, A. 2024. "Bringing True Strategic Foresight Back to Business." *Harvard Business Review*, January 12. https://hbr.org/2024/01/bringing-true-strategic-foresight-back-to-business.

Winstead, A. 2023. "Fostering a Culture of Continuous Learning in the Workplace." *Intellum*, November 16. www.intellum.com/resources/blog/continuous-learning-in-the-workplace.

Witters, D., and K. Bayne. January 18, 2024. "New Normal: Lower U.S. Life Ratings." Gallup. https://news.gallup.com/poll/548618/new-normal-lower-life-ratings-persisted-2023.aspx.

Wong, B., and K. Greenwood. 2023. "The Future of Mental Health at Work Is Safety, Community, and a Healthy Organizational Culture." *Harvard Business Review*, October 10. https://hbr.org/2023/10/the-future-of-mental-health-at-work-is-safety-community-and-a-healthy-organizational-culture.

Yu, L., and M. Zellmer-Bruhn. 2019. "What Mindfulness Can Do for a Team." *Harvard Business Review*, May 31. https://hbr.org/2019/05/what-mindfulness-can-do-for-a-team.

Zucker, R., and D. Rowell. 2021. "6 Strategies for Leading Through Uncertainty." *Harvard Business Review*, April 26. https://hbr.org/2021/04/6-strategies-for-leading-through-uncertainty.

About the Author

Michael Edmondson, PhD, is the Associate Provost for Continued Learning at the New Jersey Institute of Technology and the Vice President of the Learning and Development Initiative at the New Jersey Innovation Institute. Dr. Edmondson also serves as the Coeditor of the Human Resource Management and Organizational Behavior Collection for Business Expert Press (BEP). This is Dr. Edmondson's ninth book published by BEP.

Index